FAMILY ADVENTURE GUIDE™

PENNSYLVANIA

"The Family Adventure Guide series . . . enables parents to turn family travel into an exploration."

—Alexandra Kennedy, Editor, *FamilyFun* magazine

FAMILY ADVENTURE GUIDE™ SERIES

PENNSYLVANIA

FAMILY ADVENTURE GUIDE™

by

EMILY PAULSEN *and*
FAITH PAULSEN

A VOYAGER BOOK

The
Globe
Pequot
Press

OLD SAYBROOK, CONNECTICUT

Family Adventure Guide is a trademark of The Globe Pequot Press, Inc.
Cover and text design by Nancy Freeborn

Library of Congress Cataloging-in-Publication Data
Paulsen, Emily.
    Pennsylvania : family adventure guide / by Emily Paulsen and Faith Paulsen.
    — 1st ed.
        p.   cm.   —   (Family adventure guide series)
    "A voyager book."
    Includes index.
    ISBN 1-56440-866-3
    1. Pennsylvania—Guidebooks. 2. Family recreation—Pennsylvania—
    Guidebooks. I. Paulsen, Faith. II. Title. III. Series.
 F147.3.P38   1996
 917.4804'43—dc20
                                                            95-53717
                                                            CIP

Manufactured in the United States of America
First Edition/First Printing

To our parents, who taught us the love of travel
and the joy of discovery.

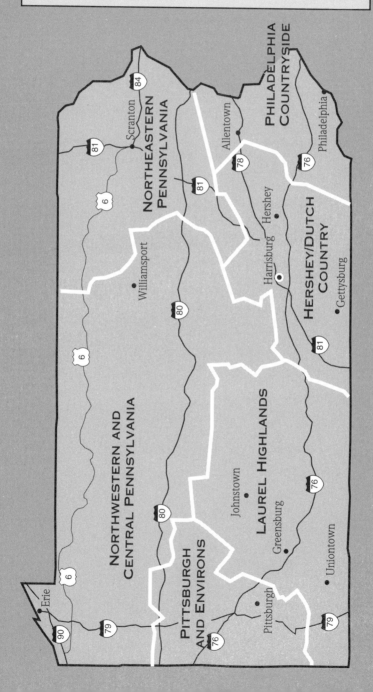

PENNSYLVANIA

NORTHEASTERN PENNSYLVANIA

PHILADELPHIA COUNTRYSIDE

HERSHEY/DUTCH COUNTRY

NORTHWESTERN AND CENTRAL PENNSYLVANIA

LAUREL HIGHLANDS

PITTSBURGH AND ENVIRONS

Scranton

Allentown

Philadelphia

Hershey

Harrisburg

Williamsport

Gettysburg

Johnstown

Greensburg

Uniontown

Pittsburgh

Erie

CONTENTS

ACKNOWLEDGMENTS

Our names may be on the cover, but there are a lot of people who have helped make this book possible. We'd like to thank all the people at the tourist boards and sites who took extra time to answer out questions and point us in the right direction. We'd also like to thank our husbands, Martin Livezey and Bart Sacks, and Faith's children, Judah, Seth, and Gideon Paulsen-Sacks for their enthusiasm and support.

INTRODUCTION

When we first visited Pennsylvania on a family vacation in 1969, neither of us realized that someday we would each adopt the state as our home, and we certainly never dreamed we would write a book about it. As children then, we saw the Liberty Bell and the Franklin Institute with our parents and our brother, Bruce. Now we take our own children to these places and many more.

Between us, we have three children—and another on the way, two dogs, and four cats. Our homes are in two different regions of Pennsylvania. Together and separately, we've enjoyed many family adventures here. But until we began to write it all down, we never fully appreciated the richness of this state.

Of course, everyone knows there's history here. Not just the Revolutionary War, but the French and Indian War, the War of 1812, Pontiac's Rebellion, the Whiskey Rebellion, and the Civil War all left their marks. Historic landmarks and living history sites can be found in every corner of the state.

The Pennsylvania state park system is truly inexhaustible. Wherever you are in the state, there's a park within 25 miles. Many have naturalists on staff during the summer and offer special environmental programs for children and families. Although some parks are day-use only, many offer camping and even a chance to stay in a log or stone cabin. Some of the cabins, built in the 1930s by the Civilian Conservation Corps, are masterpieces of craftsmanship, equipped with fireplaces, kitchenettes, and separate bedrooms—perfect for family vacationers.

Whether you're looking for a place to hike, bike, camp, ski, horseback ride, or just take a Sunday afternoon drive, Pennsylvania's got a park for you. We've tried to cover the highlights of the state park system in this book, but to devote the space each deserves, we'd have to write another book on the subject. If you want more information about Pennsylvania state parks, call their special toll-free number: (800) 63PARKS.

Pennsylvania has nine major caves open to the public, including the only water-filled cave in the country. Many of the caves offer educational programs on such topics as geology, bats, and Native American history—all geared especially for children.

In 1969, when we walked through the beating heart at the Franklin Institute, it was exciting because it was our first experience with hands-on, interactive science education. Today, the newly expanded Franklin Institute Science Museum joins a host of other "user-friendly" science centers, including the Carnegie Science Center, Williamsport's Children's Discovery Workshop, Erie's ExpERIEnce Children's Museum, and Harrisburg's up-and-coming Discovery Science Museum, to name just a few. Some of the best family adventures can be adventures in learning.

Many parents are afraid to take kids to art museums, but we've found that our children respond well to art museums as long as they experience them in small doses. Sometimes we visit the gift shop first, pick up a few postcards, then see who can find the pictured artworks in the galleries. Pennsylvania has some first-rate art museums, large and small, from the Philadelphia Museum of Art to the Carnegie Museum of Art.

No matter what the season, whether you like your adventures indoors or outdoors, Pennsylvania is a wonderful destination for families. We're certainly enjoying what the state has to offer, and we hope you will too.

The prices and rates listed in this guidebook were confirmed at press time. We recommend, however, that you call establishments to obtain current information before traveling.

Maps provided at the beginning of each chapter are for reference only and should be used in conjunction with a road map. Distances suggested are approximate.

PHILADELPHIA

In 1994, *Condé Nast Traveler* magazine rated Philadelphia "America's Friendliest City." The city of Brotherly Love may also be one of the country's "kid-friendliest" cities. Center City, where most of the city's attractions and accommodations are located, is clean, safe, and chock-full of great things for families to do and see together.

The **Philadelphia Convention and Visitors Bureau** runs special promotions and programs for families, especially in the summer. Call (800) 537–7676 to ask about current offerings. You can also request copies of the official visitors guide and the special brochure "Family Friendly Philadelphia," which details the best bets for family vacationers. You can also get up-to-the-minute information on Philadelphia from the Bureau's web site on the Internet: http://www.libertynet.org/phila-visitor.

Philadelphia is a great walking city. Most attractions are an easy jaunt from hotels and from each other. And when the feet get sore or the kids get cranky, you can always hop on the purple PHLASH bus, which stops at most of the major tourist spots downtown. To get to some of the attractions in the outskirts of the city, a car can be handy, but the one-way streets in center city and cost of parking can be frustrating. Public transportation or walking is your best bet.

Sometimes when traveling with small children, or just to get the lay of the land, an organized tour is a good idea. There are lots of companies offering tours of Philadelphia, on everything from a reproduction of an old-time trolley or a horse and buggy to a streamlined coach. Here are some companies to contact: American Trolley Tours/Choo-Choo Trolley, (215) 333–2119; Ben Franklin Carriage Co./'76 Carriage Co., (215) 923–8522, tours begin at

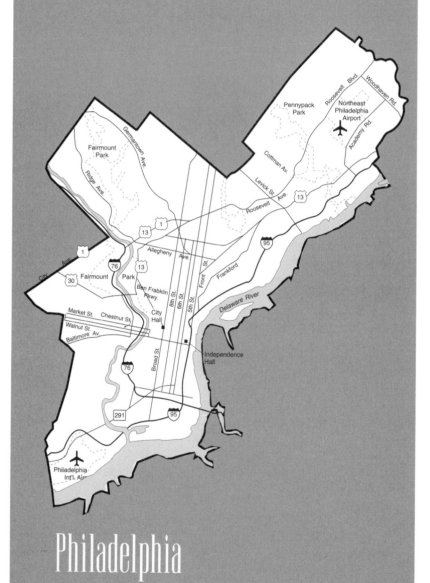

Philadelphia

Independence National Park; Gray Line Tours, (800) 577–7745/(215) 569–3666; Liberty Belle Charters, Inc., (215) 629–1131, cruises leave from Penn's Landing; Old Town Trolley, (215) 928–8687; Philadelphia Trolley Works, (215) 923–8522; PHLASH bus, (215) 4 PHLASH; Society Hill Carriage Co., (215) 627–6128, tours depart from Independence Hall.

HISTORIC PHILADELPHIA

When most people think of Philadelphia, they think of its place in United States history. You'll hear the word "first" a lot while touring this historic city. In fact, the area that makes up Independence National Historic Park is called "America's most historic square mile." Here, you'll meander the streets walked by Benjamin Franklin, Thomas Jefferson, Betsy Ross, George Washington, Dolley Madison, John Adams . . . the list goes on and on.

Forty-eight acres in Center City, comprising more than forty different historic buildings, make up **Independence National Historic Park,** including the Liberty Bell Pavilion, Independence Hall, Congress Hall, Old City Hall, Second Bank of the United States, Marine Corps Museum, Carpenters' Hall, Army-Navy Museum, Franklin Court, Christ Church, Bishop White House, Todd House, and Declaration House.

Although most people just head right for the Liberty Bell or Independence Hall, it's a good idea to start your visit to the city with a stop 2 blocks east at the **Visitor Center** (215–597–8974) located at 3rd and Chestnut streets. Here you can see *Independence,* an award-winning film directed by John Huston, and take a look at some of the special exhibits. There's also a very good bookstore and gift shop that has some great hard-to-find regional books.

While at the Visitor Center, stop at the **"Do Your Own Heritage"** kiosk. Enter your ethnic or religious background, and the computer will come up with sights and buildings in Philadelphia that are significant to your heritage.

This is also where you can sign up for **"The Liberty Tale"** walking tour, which recounts some of Philadelphia's fascinating history.

Most buildings within the park are free and open to the public, but a guide is required to tour some and for others, such as the Todd House and the Bishop White House, tickets are required. The urban park rangers of the National Park Service obviously love their jobs and they'll make history come alive with their stories of colonial Philadelphia.

Also making history come alive are the **Town Criers** and other actors in period costumes that help transport visitors back in time. A special events list distributed by the Town Criers gives a schedule of presentations, such as Ben

Franklin's Greatest Hits and the Echoes of Liberty Parade. Families are encouraged not only to watch these events, but also to participate. Most events take place on weekends, with daily performances in summer. For more information, call (800) 76–HISTORY or (215) 629–5801.

If you take the footpath across 3rd Street from the Visitor Center exit on your way toward Independence Hall, you'll pass on your left the **Second Bank of the United States** and **Carpenters' Hall,** where the First Continental Congress met in 1774. Today this building displays early carpenter's tools and chairs. Call (215) 925–0167. Carpenters' Hall is open Tuesday through Sunday 10:00 A.M. to 4:00 P.M. It is closed Tuesday in January and February. The Second Bank is open daily 9:00 A.M. to 5:00 P.M. Call (215) 925–0167 for information on Carpenters' Hall. To find out more about the Second Bank, which houses a portrait gallery, call the Visitor Center at (215) 597–8974.

The **Army-Navy Museum** and the **Marine Corps Memorial Museum** are located side-by-side on Chestnut Street. Together, these two museums offer a treasure trove for military buffs. They display uniforms, dioramas, weapons, ship models, battle flags, and other memorabilia of the U.S. armed forces, going back to the Revolution. The Army-Navy Museum features a gun deck preserved from an eighteenth-century naval ship, as well as interactive displays such as one that allows visitors to control a ship's sails and rudder. The Marine Corps Museum includes an honor roll of Marines who gave their lives in battle.

Both museums are administered by the Independence National Historic Park, and are open daily 9:00 A.M. to 5:00 P.M. Call (215) 597–8974 for information.

The **Bishop White House** and **Todd House** (located on Walnut Street between 3rd and 4th streets) present an interesting opportunity to compare and contrast two different early American life styles.

Bishop White was the first Episcopal bishop of Pennsylvania and chaplain of the Continental Congress and of the new U.S. Senate, and this elegant home was built for him and his family in 1786. Children will enjoy the boys' and girls' bedrooms, where initials were carved into the wood more than 200 years ago.

The Todd House, on the other hand, represents a middle-class Quaker home from the same period. Although well-to-do, this family lived more simply. After the death of John Todd, Dolley Todd married James Madison and became one of the most famous United States first ladies.

The Todd House and Bishop White House are open daily from 9:00 A.M. to 4:30 P.M. There is no admission charge. Tickets are required, however, and they are available at the Independence National Historic Park Visitor Center. Call (215) 597–8974.

It goes without saying that **Independence Hall** is a must-see for all ages.

FAITH AND EMILY'S FAVORITE ATTRACTIONS IN PHILADELPHIA

Franklin Institute Science Center
"Philadelphia Anthem" at Tuttleman Omniverse Theater
Academy of Natural Sciences
"Under the Mulberry Tree" near Franklin Court
Please Touch Museum
Independence Hall
Liberty Bell
Betsy Ross House
Philadelphia Zoo
Insectarium
Elfreth's Alley
Smith Playground

This building was originally known as the Pennsylvania State House, but in 1824 when General Lafayette returned to Philadelphia, he called it "the hall of independence" and the name stuck. The Declaration of Independence was adopted here, and the United States Constitution was written here, at Chestnut Street between 5th and 6th streets. The Assembly Room has been restored to look exactly as it did in 1776, and although most of the furniture is a reproduction, you can see the original inkwell in which the signers dipped their quills before putting their names to the Declaration.

Between 1790 and 1800, when Philadelphia was the capital of the United States, the Congress met in **Congress Hall** next door (215–597–8974). On the other side of Independence Hall is **Old City Hall,** where the U.S. Supreme Court met from 1791 to 1800.

The **Liberty Bell** is located in the park across the street. Young and old will want to see and touch this emblem of freedom and democracy for people all over the world. It is now housed in its own pavilion at Market Street between 5th and 6th streets.

Contrary to popular belief, the Liberty Bell's famous crack was not the result of overzealous ringing on July 4, 1776. Instead, the one-ton bell has been plagued by cracks ever since it was originally cast. It was recast twice, and then

cracked again when the bell was rung for thirty-six hours at the death of John
Marshall, Chief Justice of the Supreme Court, in 1835. Repaired once more, its
final crack occurred in 1846 on George Washington's birthday.

A couple of blocks away is **Declaration House** (or Graff House), also part
of the National Historic Park. In 1776 the Virginia delegate (Thomas Jefferson)
to the Second Continental Congress rented rooms in this building at 7th and
Market streets, and it was in these rooms that he wrote a little document called
the Declaration of Independence. School-age kids will be especially interested to
see the exact place where the Declaration was penned. The Liberty Bell Pavilion
and Declaration House are open daily 9:00 A.M. to 5:00 P.M.

On the same block, but not part of the park, are two unusual museums:
the Atwater-Kent Museum and the Balch Institute of Ethnic Studies.

The building at 15 South 7th Street was completed in 1826 and once
housed the old Franklin Institute. Today, as the **Atwater-Kent Museum,** it
tells the history of Philadelphia, a city whose story parallels that of our nation
as a whole. Philadelphia was one of the earliest cities developed with an over-
all plan, and here you can view copies of William Penn's original blueprints for
the City of Brotherly Love. Maps show how the city evolved over the years.

The Atwater-Kent Museum is open to the public at no charge, Tuesday
through Saturday 9:30 A.M. to 4:45 P.M. It is closed on Sunday, Monday, and
major holidays. Call (215) 922–3031 for a schedule of lectures, tours, and
other special activities.

The first floor of the **Balch Institute of Ethnic Studies,** at 18 South 7th
Street, is a museum of memorabilia illustrating the history of the many ethnic
groups that immigrated to Philadelphia. Kids can use a computer to key in their
ethnic background and print out a listing of Philadelphia sites related to that
ethnic group. The second floor of the institute is an extensive genealogical
research library. Both the museum and library are open Tuesday through
Saturday from 10:00 A.M. to 4:00 P.M. Admission is charged. Call (215)
925–8090 for information.

Heading north on 7th Street, you'll find the **Afro-American Historical
and Cultural Museum** at 701 Arch, a leading museum of African-American
culture. It is open Tuesday through Saturday, 10:00 A.M. to 6:00 P.M., and
Sunday, noon to 6:00 P.M. Admission is $4.00 for adults, $2.00 for children.
Call (215) 574–0380 for more information.

Walking east on Arch Street you'll pass the **Free Quaker Meeting
House Museum** and the **Christ Church Burial Ground** (at 5th and Arch)
where many Colonial and Revolutionary War heroes are buried. For good luck,
toss a penny on Benjamin Franklin's grave.

Across the street at 5th and Arch streets is the **U.S. Mint,** the world's largest coinage operation. Visitors can watch money in the making from a glass-enclosed gallery. Open daily in summer, 9:00 A.M. to 4:30 P.M.; closed Sunday in May and June and weekends September through April. Admission is free. Call (215) 597–7350 for more information.

Just 2 blocks away, on Arch between 2nd and 3rd streets, is the **Betsy Ross House.** Yes, Betsy Ross really lived here at 239 Arch Street. And yes, she really did sew flags for the Continental Congress, although nobody is certain how active a role she played in the design of the American flag. Her house was recently re-opened after renovation, and is an excellent example of a colonial artisan's home. The house is open Tuesday through Saturday 10:00 A.M. to 5:00 P.M. Admission is $1.00 for adults, 25 cents for children.

"Betsy Ross" visits the house in person, to tell her story and to demonstrate how she cuts out a five-pointed star from a folded piece of fabric with one well-placed snip of her scissors. School-age kids will find meeting this female role model a refreshing experience. For information, call (215) 627–5343.

To get an idea of what Philadelphia may have looked like in the 1700s, take a walk down **Elfreth's Alley,** the oldest residential street in America.

Take a walk back in time on the cobblestones of Elfreth's Alley, the oldest residential street in America. (Courtesy Philadelphia Convention and Visitors Bureau)

Families still inhabit this cobblestone alley tucked between Arch and Race streets on 2nd Street in Old City. Walking down this charming street, you can imagine what life must have been like when these thirty houses were built between 1728 and 1836, when carpenters and other artisans lived here. Number 126, the 1762 Mantua Maker's House Museum, is open to the public. (A mantua was a type of gown made by the house's first residents, a pair of seamstresses.) A costumed guide will show you around. On weekends in summer, there are demonstrations of traditional crafts, such as basket-weaving, broom-making, needlework, and candle-dipping. During the first weekend of June the Elfreth's Alley Association hosts Fete Days, when many of the houses and gardens are opened to the public, and Colonial crafts are demonstrated. Call (215) 574–0560 for more information.

Just about every family has somebody who wants to be a firefighter when he or she grows up. **Fireman's Hall,** at 147 North 2nd Street, will fascinate that somebody. Ever since Benjamin Franklin founded the city's first fire department in 1736, Philadelphia has had fire equipment and firefighters. You'll see old-fashioned leather buckets, hand pumpers, three fire wagons that date from 1730, a spider hose reel from 1804, fire helmets from around the world, and the scorched helmets of firefighters who died in the line of duty. Aspiring firefighters can try out the re-created living quarters of real firefighters or take the helm of a fireboat.

Fireman's Hall is in the historic district, half a block from Elfreth's Alley. It is open Tuesday through Saturday 9:00 A.M. to 5:00 P.M.; admission is free. Phone (215) 923–1438.

Walking on 2nd Street back toward the Visitor Center, stop in at **Christ Church,** between Arch and Market streets. You can find the pews occupied by George Washington, Benjamin Franklin, Betsy Ross, and other characters out of your history books. Kids will be interested to learn that this is also the birthplace of a character from a children's book: Amos, the mouse who befriended Ben Franklin in the classic *Ben and Me.* "The Nation's Church" is now celebrating 300 years as an active Episcopal parish, with Sunday morning services at 9:00 and 11:00, and Communion services on Wednesdays at noon. All are welcome to attend. The church is open to the public from 9:00 A.M. to 5:00 P.M. Monday through Saturday, and from 1:00 to 5:00 P.M. on Sunday. Call (215) 922–1695 to check winter hours and for group reservations.

Benjamin Franklin's home no longer stands at Market Street between 3rd and 4th streets, but you can still see its foundation, as well as several other houses that Franklin owned. This area has been transformed into **Franklin Court,** an interactive learning experience aimed at school-age kids that's like meeting the great man himself.

Kids can listen to the voices of such notable historic figures as John Adams, Ralph Waldo Emerson, Thomas Jefferson, Harry S Truman, Mark Twain, Lord Byron, and General Lafayette, all offering their opinions of Franklin. A series of dioramas illustrates Franklin's career, and a movie *Portrait of a Family,* tells about his family life.

When Franklin returned to Philadelphia from Paris in 1785, he used to sit under the mulberry tree—and there you can find him still, on selected performance days April through September. An especially wonderful treat for young children, "Ben Franklin" himself invites kids to gather around and listen to stories of his life. For details, contact "Ben Franklin" at P.O. Box 40178, Philadelphia 19106, call (215) 238–0871, or fax (215) 238–9102.

To enter Franklin Court, enter the archway between Market and Chestnut, in the middle of the block between 3rd and 4th streets. You can also use the walkway on Orianna Street from Chestnut Street. For information, call (215) 597–8974.

Now that you're completely steeped in history, why not eat an historic meal? Don't make the mistake of assuming **City Tavern** is just a restaurant on a colonial theme. Dining here gives a real feeling of the past. This historic gathering place, now part of the Independence National Historic Park, was opened in 1774. Paul Revere came here in May of that year to announce that the Port of Boston was closed. General Washington set up headquarters here, and Benedict Arnold slept here. John Adams called it, "the most genteel tavern in America."

The building was rebuilt in 1975 to look exactly as it did in colonial times. The tavern serves Thomas Jefferson Ale, brewed exclusively by the Dock Street Brewing Company, along with colonial specialties such as turkey-thigh stew and beef and pork pie. More tame entrées are also available.

City Tavern is in the heart of the Historic District, a short walk from Elfreth's Alley, at 138 South 2nd Street. Call (215) 413–1443.

Other sites within the Historic District include **Congregation Mikveh Israel** and the **National Museum of American Jewish History,** at 44 North 4th Street, which tells the story of the American Jewish experience. Open daily except Saturdays and Jewish holidays; admission: $2.50 adults, $1.75 children; telephone (215) 923–3811.

Rockwell fans won't want to miss the recently re-named **Curtis Center of Norman Rockwell Art** at 601 Walnut Street (215–922–4345), the largest and most complete collection of Rockwell posters, paintings, lithographs, and sketches, including the entire collection of *Saturday Evening Post* covers. There's even a recreation of Rockwell's studio, so you can see how the painter worked. The museum is open 10:00 A.M. to 4:00 P.M. Monday through Saturday, 11:00 A.M. to 4:00 P.M. Sunday year-round, except Thanksgiving,

Christmas, New Year's Day and Easter. Admission for adults is $2.00; seniors, $1.50; and children under twelve are free when accompanied by a parent.

THE WATERFRONT

The site that once hosted William Penn's arrival in 1682, **Penn's Landing** now bustles with activity, especially in fine weather. Penn's Landing is located at Market and South streets, east of Christopher Columbus Boulevard (formerly Delaware Avenue). For more information about concerts and other events at Penn's Landing, call (215) 923–8181.

Start your visit to Penn's Landing with the brand-new (opened July 1995) **Independence Seaport Museum** (211 Columbus Boulevard at Walnut Street; 215–925–5439), which uses exciting family-oriented interactive exhibits to tell the story of four centuries of maritime history. The collection of nautical artifacts and ship models that were formerly housed in the old Philadelphia Maritime Museum have now been incorporated into a panorama dominated by a model of the Benjamin Franklin Bridge, and enlivened at every turn by audiovisuals and multimedia computers. Kids can try out a sailor's berth or a rowing machine, or learn about the history of underwater exploration. Great for any folks with a taste for the nautical.

The Independence Seaport Museum also includes two real vessels: the **USS *Olympia*** and the **USS *Becuna*** (319 Delaware Avenue, at Spruce Street; 215–922–2279). Step aboard the *Olympia,* flagship of Admiral Dewey's Asiatic fleet, and see the bronze impressions of the admiral's feet in the exact spot where he stood in 1898 and said, "You may fire when you are ready, Gridley." Then take the kids aboard the *Becuna,* a guppy-class submarine from World War II where sixty-six men shared the tight living quarters.

Museum hours are 10:00 A.M. to 5:00 P.M. daily. Admission is charged. If you purchase a RiverPass, it includes round-trip fare on the Riverbus ferry from Penn's Landing to Camden, New Jersey, plus admission to both the New Jersey State Aquarium and the Independence Seaport Museum. Call (800) 634–4027 for more information. The Aquarium is worth a visit, especially if you have school-age kids. They can even pet a shark (a small, harmless one, of course).

If your family includes a "trolley jolly," then it's important to distinguish between a real trolley and a bus dressed up to look like a trolley. The **Penn's Landing Trolley** is definitely the real thing, as are the enthusiastic volunteer conductors. Board the trolley along Christopher Columbus Boulevard from Race Street to Fitzwater Street. For information, or to find out about special events such as Santa's Trolley Ride, call (215) 627–0807.

Older children or young adults will probably enjoy **Dave & Buster's.** This unusual attraction bills itself as a family entertainment center with something for everyone. However, parents should be aware that not all activities are appropriate for all ages. For example, many of the video games have violent content and may not be suitable for children. There are also bars here. Dave & Busters has taken over all 70,000 square feet of Pier 19 on the Philadelphia waterfront and filled it with skee-ball, hoop toss, video games, a variety of bars and restaurants for different tastes, music, and even "Virtuality," a virtual-reality game. You can even play golf on a virtual golf course. There's "just for fun" blackjack and poker tables, billiards, shuffleboard, and an outdoor deck with a view of the Ben Franklin Bridge.

No one under twenty-one is permitted unless accompanied by a parent. Clean and neat clothing required, no tank tops. Children are welcome, except after 10:00 P.M., which is also when the $5.00 cover charge kicks in. Individual games and activities have additional charges. Dave & Buster's is located at Pier 19 North, 325 North Columbus Boulevard, (formerly Delaware Avenue). Call (215) 413–1951 for additional details.

PARKWAY ATTRACTIONS

Philadelphia has a tradition of excellence in museums. On **Benjamin Franklin Parkway,** there's literally something for everyone—from toddlers to teenagers. We've found that for most of the museums on the Parkway, it's best to beat the crowd by arriving in the morning right when the museum opens.

If you know any dinosaur fans, be sure not to miss the **Academy of Natural Sciences** (19th and Ben Franklin Parkway). As you'll learn when you visit, this "Dinosaur Museum" played an important role in early paleontological debate. Today the first floor is crammed with dinosaur skeletons, habitat models, and informative exhibits. Near the lower entrance, on the same level with the cafeteria, is a robotic dinosaur not to be missed. It roars! On weekends, a simulated dinosaur dig lets children be paleontologists for a day.

On the third floor, "Outside In" is a hands-on exhibit for children twelve and under. Kids can touch mice, snakes, "legless lizards" (skinks), frogs, turtles, and enormous cockroaches from Madagascar. Enthusiastic and well-informed volunteers are available to answer questions.

Make sure you check the schedule when you arrive at the Academy, because there are live animal shows and films at regular intervals. Open Monday through Friday 10:00 A.M. to 4:30 P.M., weekends and selected holidays 10:00 A.M. to 5:00 P.M. Admission: Adults and children over thirteen, $5.50; seniors, $5.00; children three to twelve, $3.50; under three, free. Wheelchair accessible. Family memberships are available. Call (215) 299–1000 for more information.

If you visited the **Franklin Institute** as a child, as we did in 1969, you'll probably remember walking through the model of the human heart, following the path that the blood vessels take, hearing the sound of the heartbeat. Or maybe for you the highlight was climbing up on the real 1926 Baldwin locomotive, or sitting in the cockpit of an airplane. If you have fond memories of these exhibits, don't worry—they're still here, still delighting children. But today there's a lot more, too.

The Franklin Institute was founded in 1824, and exhibits such as the heart pioneered the idea of hands-on museum displays. The museum has continued its tradition of forward-looking exhibits with The Futures Center, added in 1992, examining science and technology of the twentieth-first century. Older children and teenagers will enjoy playing with computers and other interactive displays that teach about astronomy, medicine, botany, biology, and other sciences. Kids learn about possible career choices with videos of people from different professions talking about their work. Little ones will find many buttons to push.

Be sure to also check out the Science Center, which includes exhibits about flight, optical illusions, and the Fels Planetarium.

The Tuttleman Omniverse Theater showcases very special movie experiences on its huge screen, giving a 179-degree field of view. Check to see what movie is currently playing, but the short feature "Philadelphia Anthem," which precedes the main show, presents an excellent introduction to Philly.

The Franklin Institute is located at 20th Street and Benjamin Franklin Parkway. The Science Center is open daily 9:30 A.M. to 5:00 P.M. The Futures Center and Omniverse Theater are open Monday through Wednesday 9:30 A.M. to 5:00 P.M., Thursday through Saturday 9:30 A.M. to 9:00 P.M., and Sunday 9:30 A.M. to 6:00 P.M. Call (215) 448–1200 for prices and Omni and planetarium show times. The gift shops offer an unusual assortment of educational and scientifically oriented toys, books, posters, and so forth.

The Franklin Institute may be best for older kids, but the **Please Touch Museum,** across the street at 210 North 21st Street, is designed especially for children eight and under. Your child can visit again and again, always discovering something new.

The latest discovery is "Sendak in Philadelphia," an ingenious landscape of settings and characters from the beloved books of Maurice Sendak, including *Where the Wild Things Are* and *In the Night Kitchen.* Kids can climb onto Max's 10-foot by 6-foot bed as the walls actually turn into a jungle filled with Wild Things.

Recently recognized by *USA Today* as one of the top children's museums in the country, the Please Touch Museum is also one of the first museums to cater to small children. Children can board the cab of a real SEPTA bus or sit

Children eight and under can always discover something new at the Please Touch Museum (Courtesy Please Touch Museum)

in the driver's seat of a miniature trolley. "Foodtastic Journey" demonstrates how our food moves from the farm to the store to the kitchen. There is even a special area for the youngest visitors, ages two and under.

Adult supervision is required, and the museum specifies that no more than three children can accompany one adult. The signs posted give helpful suggestions to parents. Hours are 9:00 A.M. to 4:30 P.M. daily, 9:00 A.M. to 6:00 P.M. from July 1 to Labor Day. Admission is $6.50 ages one and over; children under one are free; seniors $5.00. Wheelchair accessible. Strollers not permitted on gallery floor. Membership available. For details, call (215) 963–0667.

Recently, the Franklin Institute teamed up with the Please Touch Museum to build the **Science Park presented by CoreStates,** a 38,000-square-foot playground with a purpose (21st Street between Winter and Race streets, adjacent to both museums). Kids can climb around on high-tech learning and play structures including a maze and three-dimensional optical illusions. Admission is free with admission to either museum.

The **Free Library of Philadelphia** (19th and Vine streets) stands across Logan Square from the Franklin Institute and the Academy of Natural Sciences, and down the Parkway from the Art Museum and Rodin Museum. It houses over six million books, magazines, newspapers, and other printed items and frequently hosts special events and exhibits. The library is open daily in winter, closed Sundays in summer. On Sundays there are tours of its remarkable rare books department. Call (215) 686–5322 for hours.

Everybody knows Rodin's "Thinker." You can see this popular sculpture at the **Rodin Museum** (22nd Street and Benjamin Franklin Parkway), along with the most complete collection of Auguste Rodin's work outside Paris. This museum is administered by the Philadelphia Museum of Art down the Parkway, and is open Tuesday through Sunday, 10:00 A.M. to 5:00 P.M. Voluntary donations are requested. Guided tours are given on the first and third Saturdays of the month at 1:00 P.M. Call (215) 684–7788.

At the far end of the Parkway, on the other side of Eakins Oval, are some steps that many people will recognize. Who can forget that memorable scene from *Rocky* when the boxer runs up all these steps? But the collection inside the **Philadelphia Museum of Art** is even more memorable—over 40,000 works of art, including one of the largest and most important collections of European art in the United States. The art museum takes a somewhat unusual approach, juxtaposing the painting, sculpture, furniture, ceramics, textiles, and architectural elements from the same period to convey a sense of that time. The museum is also known for its outstanding collection of rural Pennsylvania crafts and works by Thomas Eakins. We know a seven-year-old boy who could spend all day in the "Arms and Armor" collection.

The Art Museum's neo-Classical facade stands at the end of Benjamin Franklin Parkway at 26th Street, within walking distance (unless your children's legs are very short) of the Franklin Institute, Free Library of Philadelphia, Please Touch Museum, Logan Circle and other parkway sites.

The museum is open Tuesday through Sunday 10:00 A.M.to 5:00 P.M., on Wednesdays until 8:45 P.M. Admission is charged, except on Sunday mornings from 10:00 A.M. to 1:00 P.M. Free guided tours are conducted hourly between 11:00 A.M. and 3:00 P.M. Tours are also available in foreign languages (215–684–7923) and sign language (215–684–7601). The museum restaurant is open Tuesday through Sunday 11:45 A.M. to 2:15 P.M. and Wednesday 5:00 P.M. to 7:30 P.M. The cafeteria is open 10:00 A.M. to 3:30 P.M. weekdays only. Call (215) 763–8100 for further information.

"Something every Sunday" is how the museum describes its family activities. Different programs are offered, usually on a walk-in basis, for families with children ages three to twelve. Most of the programs take place on Sundays at 11:30 A.M. or 1:30 P.M. so that you can take advantage of the Sunday morning free admission. Programs range from story-telling to hands-on art activities, with titles like "Tales and Treasures," "Try a Technique" and "Gallery Games." Many of these programs are free and the rest are $1.00 for children of members, $2.00 for children of non-members. Accompanying adults are free. Every

FAITH AND EMILY'S FAVORITE EVENTS IN PHILADELPHIA

"Kids' Day" at Sunoco Welcome America! Celebration (July) (215) 636–1666 or (800) 537–7676

Mummer's Day Parade (January 1, summer version in June) (215) 336–3050

"Philadelphia Freedom Spectacular" at Independence Seaport Museum (July) (215) 470–1176

Summer Concerts at Penn's Landing (June through August) (215) 636–1666

Philadelphia International Theater Festival for Children (last week of May) (215) 898–6791 or 898–6683

Philadelphia Flower Show (late February through early March) (215) 625–8253

Daily News Presents "Yo! Philadelphia" (Labor Day weekend) (215) 636–1666

day of the week you can pick up a family oriented self-guided tour brochure at the West Information Desk. The museum's automated information line is (215) 684–7500. For information about family activities and children's art classes, call (215) 684–7605.

In 1842 when Charles Dickens visited the United States, there were two sights he didn't want to miss: Niagara Falls and the **Eastern State Penitentiary.** It has been called the most influential prison in the world, because its design was grounded on the nineteenth century's most modern ideas about civic responsibility and criminal behavior. Al Capone did time here, as did the "gentleman bandit" Willie Sutton. An operating prison for more than 140 years, until 1971, the building has recently been re-opened as the Eastern State Penitentiary Task Force makes plans for its future. Today there are special art exhibits here, and sometimes dramatic productions.

The building has been made safe for tours, but has otherwise been left "as is." Visitors must wear hard hats and stay with tour groups. Most people won't have to be reminded; the decaying plaster, dampness, and remnants of prison life make this a pretty eerie place—great for teenagers!

The penitentiary is located on Fairmount Avenue at 22nd Street, 3 blocks from the Philadelphia Museum of Art and the parkway. It is open to the public May through October, Thursday through Sunday from 10:00 A.M. to 7:00 P.M. Guided tours are available every hour from 10:00 A.M. to 6:00 P.M. Children under seven are not admitted. For information about special events and to check hours and admission prices, call (215) 236–7236 or 568–8225.

At 8,700 acres, Philadelphia's **Fairmount Park** is one of the world's largest city parks and an amazing source of activities. The park includes the Philadelphia Museum of Art, Philadelphia Zoo, Andorra Natural Area, Bartram's Gardens, Boathouse Row, Fairmount Waterworks, Horticulture Center, Japanese House and Gardens, Memorial Hall, Ohio House, Ryerss Library and Museum, as well as the ten Mansions of Fairmount Park.

Andorra Natural Area (Northwestern Avenue, in Fairmount Park) offers many wonderful programs for children including nature trails, exhibits, and special events. Open daily; call (215) 685–9285.

Bartram's Historic Garden (54th Street and Lindbergh Boulevard), the oldest surviving botanical garden in the country, includes the pre-Revolutionary home of botanist John Bartram, as well as forty-four acres of gardens. The garden is free and open daily from dawn to dusk. The home is open Wednesday through Sunday noon to 4:00 P.M. There is a charge for the house tour: adults $3.00, children under twelve $2.00. Call (215) 729–5281.

A lovely place for a stroll along the Schuylkill River, **Boathouse Row** consists of twelve nineteenth-century buildings where Philadelphia's rowing clubs keep their boats. The outline of each boathouse is trimmed with lights, to create a luminous view of the boathouses from across the river at night.

One little-known attraction in Fairmount Park is **Smith Playground and Playhouse;** if you have children under age ten or so, be sure to check this one out. The Giant Slide, for example, built in 1908, proves that kids really haven't changed that much in their enjoyment of outdoor equipment. The playground is located behind the driving range at 33rd and Oxford streets, in the Strawberry Mansion section of Fairmount Park.

In Fairmount Park, you can also discover the **Philadelphia Marionette Theater and Museum** on Belmont Mansion Drive. Call (215) 879–1213.

The **Fairmount Park Information Center** is located at Memorial Hall, North Concourse Drive near 42nd Street and Parkside Avenue (215) 685–0000. (The building is also police headquarters.) For information about the mansions, including the trolley tour, please contact Mansions of Fairmount Park, Park House Guides Office, Philadelphia Museum of Art, or call (215) 684–7926.

The **Philadelphia Zoo** (3400 West Girard Avenue; (215–243–1100) offers a treat for all ages—a chance to meet over 1,500 animals housed in naturalistic settings, all surrounded by beautiful trees and plantings. The zoo, a must-see for families with young children visiting Philadelphia, includes the Treehouse, Children's Zoo, Carnivore Kingdom, Bear Country, and Reptile House. Open daily 9:30 A.M. to 5:00 P.M. Adults $8.50, seniors and children ages two to eleven $6.00, members and children under two free.

Philadelphians' love for their zoo was recently dramatized by the outpouring of support following the December 24, 1995 fire that destroyed the World of Primates exhibit, killing twenty-three beloved animals.

THE REST OF PHILADELPHIA

Philadelphia's mayor, Edward G. Rendell, realizes the importance of tourism to his city. One of his first actions upon taking office was to start renovating the amazing **City Hall** (at the intersection of Broad and Market streets, the dead center of William Penn's original plan for the city) and open it for free tours. See the courtroom where the film *Philadelphia* was made and the 548-foot-tall tower that is topped by a statue of William Penn. When the Phillies became the National League champions in 1994, maintenance workers placed a baseball cap on Penn's head. The observation deck (at William Penn's feet) affords a spectacular view of the city. Tours leave every fifteen minutes from 10:00 A.M. to 3:00 P.M. weekdays. For more information call (215) 569–3187.

While you're in the neighborhood, drop by the **Philadelphia Visitors Center** at 16th Street and JFK. For information about free historical musical theater productions, costumed town criers, "The Liberty Tale," and "Under the Mulberry Tree," call (800) HISTORY or (215) 628–5801. You'll also want to check out two sculptures for which Philadelphia is famous: Claes Oldenburg's Clothespin located in Centre Square Plaza at 15th and Walnut streets; and Robert Indiana's Philadelphia LOVE at Kennedy Plaza, located at 15th Street and JFK.

Walking up Broad Street near Cherry, 1 block from City Hall and the Convention Center, you can't miss the graceful front staircase of the **Academy of Fine Arts,** home of the nation's first art museum, the **Museum of American Art of Pennsylvania,** and its first art school, the **Academy School.** The building (118 North Broad Street at Cherry; 215–972–7600, with its Gothic arches and lacy ironwork, is a masterpiece of High Victorian Gothic architecture. The museum collection includes works by Benjamin West, Charles Willson Peale (one of the Academy's founders), Thomas Eakins (who served as the Academy's director during the 1880s), Mary Cassatt, Winslow Homer, Horace Pippin, Andrew Wyeth, Alexander Calder, Louise Nevelson, and many others.

You can make your visit more lively with Family Inform, an audio guide system. Look around the galleries to find numbers that you key into the audio machine's keypad, and you can hear messages about the works of art.

The museum is open Monday through Saturday, 10:00 A.M. to 5:00 P.M., and on Sunday from 11:00 A.M. to 5:00 P.M., closed New Year's Day, Thanksgiving and Christmas. Admission is $5.95 for adults, $3.95 for children under twelve, $4.95 for seniors and students with ID, and free to members and children under five.

Broad Street south of City Hall has recently been renamed the "Avenue of the Arts." Already home to the Academy of Music, the Merriam Theater, and the University of the Arts, several new theaters are planned for the street.

That spectacular opera house seen in the movie *The Age of Innocence* is Philadelphia's own **Academy of Music.** You can see the landmark if you attend a concert by the **Philadelphia Orchestra** or a performance by the **Opera Company of Philadelphia.** But for $3.00, you can take a one-hour afternoon tour of this beloved building on Broad and Locust streets, including a peek backstage and into the artists' dressing rooms. Call (215) 893–1935 for tour dates or to make reservations.

If you're hungry and you don't know what to eat, or if you're planning a picnic, stop by the **Reading Terminal Market** (12th and Arch streets; 215–922–2317) where farmers and merchants from around the Philadelphia area (many of them Amish) sell very fresh produce, cheese, fish, meats, baked goods, and much more. There are hundreds of stalls to browse through, so each member of the family is sure to find something delicious.

While you're at the market, head across the street and up the stairs to the old Reading Terminal, which has recently been converted as part of the **Pennsylvania Convention Center.** This cavernous hall was once the main train station in downtown Philadelphia.

One block east and you're in the heart of Philadelphia's **Chinatown.** Stop here for authentic Chinese cuisine and products. Chinatown is located between Arch and Vine streets, 11th to 8th streets. For information about Chinatown, call (215) 922–2156.

A couple of long blocks north is the house where Edgar Allan Poe lived with his wife and mother-in-law in 1843. In this home at 7th and Spring Garden streets, Poe entertained some of the leading literary figures of the time. There is a brief slide presentation about the author's life. The **Edgar Allen Poe National Memorial** is open 9:00 A.M. to 5:00 P.M. daily, except Christmas and New Year's Day. Admission is free. Call (215) 597–8780 for details.

To get a feeling for a traditional, stately Philadelphia neighborhood, stroll around the blocks surrounding **Rittenhouse Square.** At 2010 Delancey Place on Rittenhouse Square, the **Rosenbach Museum and Library** (215–732–

1600) houses an astounding collection of rare books, manuscripts, antique furniture, silver, porcelain, and works of art in the beautiful home of the Rosenbach brothers, who lived here from 1928 until their deaths in 1952 and 1953. This wonderful museum is more suited to older children and literary folks, although occasionally there are special exhibits of illustrated books that may appeal to youngsters. Rittenhouse Row runs from 21st Street to Broad Street and from Spruce to Sansom.

Among the over 30,000 rare books and 300,000 manuscripts are letters penned by George Washington, Thomas Jefferson, Benjamin Franklin, and Abraham Lincoln. You can also see Lewis Carroll's own copy of *Alice in Wonderland,* the manuscript for James Joyce's *Ulysses,* and the notes for Bram Stoker's *Dracula.* The museum also owns over 3,000 original drawings by Maurice Sendak, noted author of classic children's books.

Open Tuesday through Sunday 11:00 A.M. to 4:00 P.M. (last tour, 2:45 P.M.). Closed Monday, national holidays, and the month of August. Admission $3.50, discounts available for students and seniors.

A couple of blocks away, the **Civil War Library and Museum** (1805 Pine Street, 215–735–8196) houses artifacts from that tumultuous era in our history.

Philadelphia is home to a huge number of colleges and universities. Besides adding to the rich cultural diversity of the city, these institutions offer some unusual museums. For example, check out the **Temple University Dental Museum** (Broad Street and Alleghany Avenue; 215–221–2816).

Also in this area of North Philadelphia, the **Wagner Free Institute** (1700 West Montgomery Avenue; 215–763–6529) presents an unusual opportunity to visit a science museum that looks pretty much the way it did in about 1865. Amateur scientist William Wagner used his collection of over 10,000 specimens to illustrate his lectures, and here they remain, enclosed in the same glass cases: Wagner's fossils, minerals, and skeletons of many creatures, including dinosaurs and insects. This is a great place for amateur naturalists and paleontologists. Open Tuesday through Friday 10:00 A.M. to 4:00 P.M. for self-guided tours. Admission is free.

A unique diversion, the **Foot Museum** at the Pennsylvania College of Podiatric Medicine, 8th and Race streets, displays footwear belonging to celebrities such as Ringo Starr, Julius Erving, Lucille Ball, Mamie Eisenhower, and Ronald and Nancy Reagan. There are also shoes from around the world, old books on foot care, and other curiosities. Free tours can be arranged in advance by calling (215) 629–0300.

The **University Museum** (at the University of Pennsylvania, 33rd and Spruce streets) is a treasure trove for your budding archaeologist or anyone interested in sphinxes, mummies, African sculpture, or ancient Mayan, Roman, or Polynesian culture. The three floors of this museum are crammed with a wealth of artifacts unearthed by the University Museum's own world-renowned archaeological and ethnographic expeditions.

Kids will be awe-struck by the genuine Sphinx of Rameses II, weighing in at twelve tons of solid granite. They will be mystified, and perhaps a little unnerved, by the real mummies. Other ongoing exhibits include "Ancient Mesopotamia: The Royal Tombs of Ur," and "Raven's Journey: World of Alaska's Native People." For details, call (215) 898–4000. The University Museum is open Tuesday through Saturday, 10:00 A.M. to 4:30 P.M. and Sunday 1:00 to 5:00 P.M. It is closed Sundays in the summer. Admission is $5.00 for adults, $2.50 for students and children. Children under six are free.

At the College of Physicians of Philadelphia (not an educational institution but an organization of doctors), there's the **Mutter Museum** of medical anomalies (19 South 22nd Street; 215–563–3737). A wall of more than one hundred skulls, the tumor removed from President Cleveland's jaw, and the preserved body of an eighteenth-century woman are among the ghoulish artifacts here. What teenager could resist? The Mutter Museum is open Tuesday through Friday 10:00 A.M. to 4:00 P.M. Admission is $2.00 for adults and children over six, $1.00 for seniors.

Also on the Penn campus, kids might enjoy a look at College Hall, one of two Philadelphia structures reputed to be a model for the Addams Family house. (Charles Addams went to Penn, and was well acquainted with this building. The other candidate is the Ebeneezer Maxwell Mansion.) There are also some interesting sculptures on this campus, such as Claes Oldenburg's oversized button and the statue of Benjamin Franklin.

Speaking of pleasing teenagers, or sports fans of any age, Philadelphia has several professional and amateur teams whose games provide terrific family outings. The **Eagles** and the **Phillies** play at **Veterans Stadium** (Phillies: 215–463–1000; Eagles: 215–463–5500). The **CoreStates Spectrum** offers basketball (the **76ers**: 215–339–7600), ice hockey (the **Flyers**: 215–465–4500), indoor lacrosse (the **Wings**), and roller hockey (the **Bulldogs**). Call the Spectrum at (215) 336–3600 for more information. Veterans Stadium and the Spectrum are located across the street from each other in South Philadelphia, at Broad Street and Pattison Avenue.

South Philadelphia is home to many of the city's ethnic neighborhoods, as well as the world's largest outdoor market, the **Italian Market** (9th Street, between Warton and Christian streets; 215–922–5557). It's a great place to find unusual cheeses, fresh fruits and vegetables, homemade pasta, exotic spices, and unusual kitchen wares.

No Philadelphian can hear the tune of "Golden Slippers" without pictur-ing the sequined costumes, the feathers, and of course, the distinctive "strut" of the Mummers. But non-Philadelphians may need a word of explanation. A phenomenon unique to Philadelphia, Mummery is centered around the an-nual Philadelphia New Year's Day Parade, when the string bands, fancy brigades, and clowns strut down Broad Street. The **Mummers Museum** (1100 South 2nd Street) surrounds you with the spangles, the colors, the his-tory, and the music of the Mummers. You can see videos of past parades, learn how the costumes are made, and practice your "Mummers' Strut."

The museum is open Tuesday through Saturday from 9:30 A.M. to 5:00 P.M., and Sunday from 12:00 noon to 5:00 P.M. It is closed on Monday, and on Sundays in July and August. Admission is charged, and guided tours are avail-able by reservation. Call (215) 336–3050.

In 1777, a chain of tree trunks was hung across the Delaware River between **Fort Mifflin** on the Pennsylvania side and Fort Mercer on the Delaware side. The purpose was to prevent the British from sailing up the river to deliver supplies to their troops. When the British fired on Fort Mifflin, the 450 men there valiantly held off the British fleet for forty days, hopelessly delaying them.

Although Fort Mifflin was rebuilt in the 1800s, many of its Revolutionary walls still stand, and it still has its original moat. On Sunday afternoons, in addi-tion to tours, there are militia guard drills. A blacksmith also demonstrates how weapons were made in this period.

Fort Mifflin is located on Fort Mifflin Road. Open April through November, Wednesday through Sunday, 10:00 A.M. to 4:00 P.M. During the off-season, pre-booked tours may be available. Call (215) 492–3395 or 365–9781.

Although located within Philadelphia's city limits, the Manayunk and Chestnut Hill sections feel more like small towns than urban neighborhoods. **Manayunk,** one of the country's oldest villages, has a reputation as an artists' community. **Chestnut Hill** has a different atmosphere, with its beautiful old homes and elegant shops. Both offer wonderful restaurants.

Rumor has it that the **Ebeneezer Maxwell Mansion** is the model for the Addams Family House, as depicted by Philadelphia's own Charles Addams. It is unclear how much the cartoonist Charles Addams was influenced by the Victorian buildings he saw, but it is known that he was familiar with both College Hall (on the Penn campus) and the Ebeneezer Maxwell Mansion, and both may have shaped the architecture of the Addams Family house. This eigh-teen-room Victorian mansion in the Chestnut Hill section was built in 1859. Young children will love the children's bedroom filled with games and toys of the period. The gadgets are also wonderful, including an apple corer and a sausage stuffer. The gardens include a grape arbor and a small pond.

The Mansion is at Greene and Tulpehocken streets; telephone (215) 438–1861. At Christmas there's a "Dickensian Christmas" celebration and in the summer, a "Victorian Ice Cream Social." Open Wednesday through Sunday 1:00 P.M. to 5:00 P.M.

The **Morris Arboretum** is the botanical garden of the University of Pennsylvania, filled with exotic plants and picturesque vistas. The Arboretum fills ninety-two acres in Chestnut Hill, including Japanese gardens, rose gardens, the only Victorian fernery in the United States, and a charming pond complete with swans. It is located on Germantown Pike at 100 Northwestern Avenue. Open daily 10:00 A.M. to 4 P.M. Guided tours are given Saturday and Sunday at 2:00 P.M. Adults $3.00, students and seniors $1.50, and children under six free. Call (215) 247–5777 for more information.

Kids love bugs, even if their parents don't. Steve's Bug-Off Exterminating Co. has assembled the **Insectarium** (at 8046 Frankford Avenue in Northeast Philadelphia; 215–338–3000), a collection of live insects in naturalized settings, mounted specimens, and interactive displays. This one-of-a-kind museum is designed to teach the importance of insects as part of the diversity of nature—but mostly it's a lot of fun. You won't be able to forget the "cockroach kitchen," the live termite tunnel, or the tarantulas (no matter how hard you try). The Insectarium is open 10:00 A.M. to 4:00 P.M., Monday through Saturday. Admission to the Insectarium is $3.00 for children two and older. It is free for anyone younger than two.

Another way to enjoy the natural world is a stop at **John Heinz National Wildlife Refuge,** where there are butterflies, geese, pheasants, woodcocks, egrets, muskrats, turtles, frogs, deer, and wildflowers galore. This is a great place to hike, bike, or canoe (bring your own canoe), but first, visit the Visitor Contact Station for information and advice. For many families, the 3-mile East Impoundment Trail is the best choice. Don't forget your binoculars to enhance the view from the Observation Tower. The Wildlife Refuge is located in the Tinicum section at 86th Street and Lindbergh Boulevard. Call (215) 365–3118 for more information.

PHILADELPHIA COUNTRYSIDE

The area surrounding Philadelphia offers a wealth of opportunities for family adventure. Living history sites such as Hopewell Furnace, Colonial Pennsylvania Plantation, and Peter Wentz Farmstead bring kids face-to-face with the past. Theme parks such as Sesame Place and Dorney Park and Wildwater Kingdom bring the family together with rides, shows, and water slides for all ages. The Barnes Foundation's collection of Impressionist art is dazzling. The streets of New Hope teem with art galleries, craft shops, and restaurants. Historic parks such as the Brandywine Battlefield, Washington Crossing, and Valley Forge offer a great combination of history and outdoor fun, all in the beautiful Pennsylvania countryside.

BRANDYWINE VALLEY

For a trip that includes historic homes and battlefields, art, gardens, and a mushroom museum, all within easy distance of each other, contact the **Brandywine Valley Tourist Information Center** (P.O. Box 910, Department 9, Kennett Square PA 19348; 800–228–9933).

Longwood Gardens, on Route 1 in Kennett Square, is a place to enjoy the variety of nature, both indoors and out. With a four-acre conservatory, Longwood's visitors can see orchids, roses, bonsai, exotic jungle plants, and waterfalls, even on the coldest winter days. And on warmer days, you can tour the outside gardens and the fountains. No matter what the weather, don't miss the annual holiday topiary display.

Longwood Gardens is open 9:00 A.M. to 6:00 P.M. daily. Call (610) 388–1000 for information. The gardens are open many evenings for special events; call (610) 388–6741 for a complete schedule. Admission is charged. The

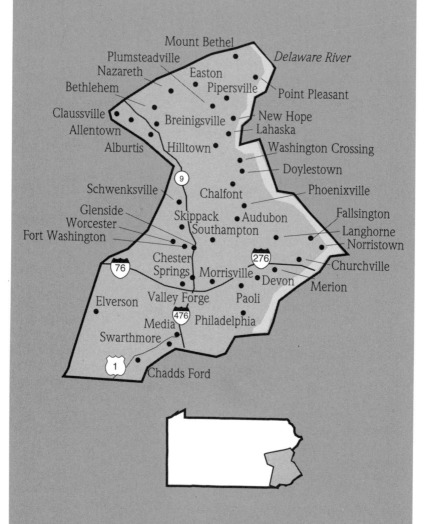

Mount Bethel
Plumsteadville
Nazareth
Easton
Bethlehem
Pipersville
Delaware River
Point Pleasant
Claussville
Breinigsville
New Hope
Allentown
Lahaska
Alburtis
Hilltown
Washington Crossing
Schwenksville
Chalfont
Doylestown
Phoenixville
Glenside
Skippack
Audubon
Fallsington
Worcester
Southampton
Langhorne
Fort Washington
Norristown
Chester Springs
Morrisville
Churchville
Devon
Elverson
Valley Forge
Paoli
Merion
Media
Philadelphia
Swarthmore
Chadds Ford

9

76

276

476

1

Philadelphia Countryside

Terrace Restaurant includes both a cafeteria and a sit-down dining room. Reservations are recommended for the dining room.

They call it the "mushroom capital of the world." Kennett Square grows more mushrooms than any other area. One-half mile south of Longwood Gardens, **Phillips Mushroom Place** is actually a working mushroom farm, where many different varieties of mushrooms are grown. The museum tells how the ancient Egyptians believed that the mushroom would make them immortal, and the Romans reserved mushrooms for the exclusive use of royalty. Fresh mushrooms are available in the gift shop. Phillips Mushroom Place is located on U.S. Route 1, 909 East Baltimore Pike, Kennett Square. Call (610) 388–6082 for details. Admission prices are very reasonable: adults, $1.25; seniors, 75 cents; children seven to twelve, 50 cents; children six and under, free.

The fields, mills, and farms of rural Pennsylvania have found their way into the art of Chadds Ford's most famous artist, Andrew Wyeth. Here, you're surrounded by Wyeth's landscapes and his art. You can visit the historic Brandywine Battlefield, eat lunch in an historic inn, shop, and take a walk along the Brandywine River.

Andrew Wyeth came from a family of distinguished artists. The **Brandy-wine River Museum,** in a converted gristmill on Route 1 in Chadds Ford, has the world's largest collection of Andrew Wyeth's work, as well as that of his father, N.C. Wyeth, his son, Jamie Wyeth, and other family members. Many visitors will recognize the illustrations of N.C. Wyeth for such swash-buckling classics as *Treasure Island* and *Kidnapped.* For details, call (610) 388–2700.

After you enjoy the artwork in the museum, your family might enjoy a walk along the river. The museum is administered by the Brandywine Conservancy, an environmental group. The Conservancy maintains a nature trail starting at the museum. Within walking distance, you may rent a canoe or inner tube, or visit **John Chads House.** On Sundays, you can watch bread being baked in the beehive oven. The house is open during the summer, Friday through Sunday from noon to 5:00 P.M. Call (610) 388–7376.

Chadds Ford Village is a charming place to browse in craft shops, or to enjoy a meal at the **Chadds Ford Inn,** which has been serving travellers since 1736. Telephone: (610) 388–7361.

At the **Barns-Brinton House** on Route 1, guides in period costume demonstrate colonial crafts and give tours of this eighteenth-century home and tavern. The house is open weekends from May to September, noon to 6:00 P.M. (610–388–7376). Just past the herb garden, you'll find the **Chaddsford Winery.** The winery is open Tuesday through Saturday 10:00 A.M. to 5:30 P.M. and Sunday from noon to 5:00 P.M. From April through January, the winery expands its hours to Monday from 10:00 A.M. to 5:30 P.M. and Friday from

10:00 A.M. to 7:00 P.M. You can also see winemaking demonstrations on Saturday from 10:00 A.M. to 5:30 P.M., and Sunday noon to 5:00 P.M.

After retreating at the Battle of Brandywine, George Washington's troops moved on to camp at Valley Forge. At the **Brandywine Battlefield,** you can tour the house where Washington set up his headquarters. The Visitors Center offers an audiovisual introduction to the park, along with maps for a self-guided driving tour that includes twenty-eight historic points of interest. The battlefield is open year-round Tuesday through Saturday 9:00 A.M. to 5:00 P.M., and Sunday noon to 5:00 P.M.; picnic areas are available. Telephone: (610) 459–3342.

ELVERSON

Watch a real blacksmith hammering a shape from hot iron. Visit a cast house where iron weapons were made for the Continental Army. Learn how colonists prepared food and clothing. **Hopewell Furnace National Historic Site** gives you a chance to see what life was like in a colonial iron-making town. As you take your self-guided walking tour, taped messages give you a first-hand feeling for the experiences of the people who lived and worked here. Although open year-round, the site is most active in summer when authentically costumed artisans demonstrate their crafts. Located at 2 Mark Bird Lane in Elverson; open daily 9:00 A.M. to 5:00 P.M., except Thanksgiving, Christmas, and New Year's Day. Handicapped-accessible. Call (610) 582–8773, TDD 582–2093.

Nearby, **French Creek State Park** offers outdoor family adventures such as hiking, fishing, swimming, and camping, as well as winter sports. You may wish to have lunch or do some shopping in Victorian **St. Peter's Village.**

CHESTER SPRINGS

Where nature brought forth yellow water with medicinal properties, man has brought forth *The Blob.* Some would say Chester Springs' attractions have run "from the sublime to the ridiculous."

For centuries, starting with indigenous peoples and later colonial settlers, presidents, and entertainers, people have come to **Yellow Springs** in hopes of a cure to their illnesses. In 1722, there was a health spa here. From 1916 to 1952 the Pennsylvania Academy of Fine Arts ran a landscape school on these beautiful grounds. And later still, Valley Forge Films made movies here, including the 1958 Steve McQueen classic *The Blob* and *4-D Man.*

Today this site is operated as **Historic Yellow Springs, Inc.,** located on Art School Road in Chester Springs. Visitors may tour the grounds and village, participate in special programs such as art classes and workshops, or attend annual events such as the "Frolicks." For information, call (610) 827–7414.

VALLEY FORGE

The nice thing about **Valley Forge National Historic Park** is its mixture of history and outdoor fun.

After viewing the eighteen-minute introductory film and exhibits at the Visitor Center (at State Route 23 and North Gulph Road), you can get information about touring the park. There are so many different ways to enjoy Valley Forge, you can choose the one that's just right for your family. From April to October, tour buses take a regular route, allowing visitors to get off when a particular site sparks their interest, and then catch the next bus. A map allows families to take a self-guided driving tour, narrated by audiotape if desired. Six miles of trails are available for those who prefer to see the park by bike, on foot, or on horseback. There are fields perfect for kite-flying and three different picnic areas. The first encampment site on the auto tour, just past the visitor center, has some great hills for sledding.

No matter how you go, your kids will not want to miss the re-created encampment where Washington's troops spent the winter of 1777–78. And it may be sexist to say so, but boys are especially interested in the Artillery Park, reconstructed fortifications, and the **Grand Parade Grounds,** where the troops trained for battle. General Washington set up his temporary headquarters in **Isaac Potts' House** (also known as **Washington's Headquarters**), now restored to look as it did during that famous winter.

The **Washington Memorial Chapel,** on park grounds but privately operated, commemorates the Revolutionary War and the armed forces. Also privately operated, the **Valley Forge Historical Society Museum** on Route 23; 610–783–0535) exhibits a collection of Revolutionary War memorabilia.

Valley Forge National Historic Park buildings are open daily except Christmas, from 9:00 A.M. until 5:00 P.M. The self-guided driving tour is open all year from 6:00 A.M. to 10:00 P.M. Accessibility for the disabled is available in most areas of the park by inquiring at the Visitor Center Information Desk. The park hosts special events on Washington's Birthday, the anniversary of the march into Valley Forge (December 19), and the anniversary of the march out (June 19).

For another kind of family adventure in the Valley Forge area, contact **United States Hot Air Balloon Company,** P.O. Box 490, Hopewell Road, St. Peters 10470; (800) 76–FLY US.

AUDUBON

Although John James Audubon lived at **Mill Grove** for only three years, it was his first home in America (he arrived here in 1804), and the perfect place to inspire his career as a painter of birds. One hundred and seventy acres of greenery and 180 species of birds surround the house, built in 1762. This is a lovely spot to stroll

At Valley Forge National Historic Park, you can see the encampment where George Washington's troops spent the famous winter of 1777–78. (Courtesy Valley Forge Convention & Visitors Bureau)

in the woods or enjoy a peaceful view of Perkiomen Creek. Inside the home, you may tour eleven rooms filled with Audubon's collection of paintings, stuffed birds, and birds' eggs. The museum also owns a complete set of Audubon's greatest work, *The Birds of America,* with each bird painted in actual size.

Mill Grove is located in Audubon at Audubon and Pawlings roads. Open Tuesday through Sunday, 10:00 A.M. to 4 P.M., free of charge. Call (610) 666–5593.

PAOLI

What is it about the Philadelphia area that seems to breed unforgettable characters? Doylestown has Henry Mercer, Merion has Albert Barnes, and Paoli has Wharton Esherick.

Wharton Esherick started out as a painter, but after moving in 1913 to a stone farmhouse near Paoli, he became fascinated with wood. The **Wharton Esherick Studio** reflects this fascination. Everywhere you look, you discover some whimsical wooden object: wooden sculptures, wooden picture frames, wooden furniture.

Esherick was also entranced by what is now called "found objects." The handrail of his astounding double-spiral staircase is a real mastodon tusk! The artist created chairs out of hammer handles or wagon wheels.

Reservations are required for one-hour tours of Esherick's home and studio. Tours are available March through December, Saturdays 10:00 A.M. to 5:00 P.M. and Sundays 1:00 to 5:00 P.M. For directions and reservations, call (610) 644–5822.

PHOENIXVILLE

Water World, on Route 724 in Phoenixville, is a relaxing place to cool off on a sticky summer day, with three water slides, a large pool, and a wading pool for the little ones. Call (610) 935–1290 for details.

NORRISTOWN

A real kid-friendly zoo, **Elmwood Park Zoo** has a duck pond, petting zoo, cougars, deer, bison, gibbons, and more. We found that even a toddler with short legs can walk the whole thing without crying to be carried or feeling overwhelmed. The zoo is located at Harding Boulevard in Norristown's Elmwood Park, with a playground nearby. Call (610) 277–DUCK. Admission is free, but donations are gladly accepted.

DEVON

There are children's theater productions and other performances at **Valley Forge Music Fair,** located near the Devon exit of Route 202. For information, call (610) 644–5000 or 296–9820.

MEDIA

On an eighteenth-century farm, animals were left to graze freely, not penned up as they are today. In the root cellar the farmer's family stored carrots, onions, and potatoes and in the springhouse flowing water cooled milk and eggs. The clothing was made by hand, spun of natural fibers. All these details are meticulously recreated at **Colonial Pennsylvania Plantation.**

This is actually a working farm where 120 acres of crops are grown using methods that date back more than 200 years. Here you can observe the staff demonstrating cooking, spinning, weaving, sheep-shearing, planting, and harvesting. Located in beautiful **Ridley Creek State Park,** the farm is open weekends, April to November, 10:00 A.M. to 4:00 P.M. Call (610) 566–1725.

Also in the park, the adjacent **Tyler Arboretum** has an extensive collection of native and non-native plants. Highlights include a giant sequoia with a circumference of 9 feet and a unique fragrant garden designed specifically for the visually impaired. The arboretum is open daily at no charge, 8:00 A.M. until dusk. Call (610) 566–5431.

FAITH AND EMILY'S FAVORITE ATTRACTIONS IN THE PHILADELPHIA COUNTRYSIDE

Sesame Place
Colonial Pennsylvania Plantation
Childventure Museum
Valley Forge National Park
Mercer Museum
Dorney Park & Wildwater Kingdom
Tubing at Point Pleasant
Elmwood Park Zoo

SWARTHMORE

One hundred and ten acres surrounding Swarthmore College constitute the college's **Scott Arboretum.** Come here for a quiet stroll through collections of flowering cherries, roses, conifers, daffodils, dogwoods, lilacs, hollies, rhododendrons, and more. Specialty gardens include the Theresa Long Garden of Fragrance, the Dean Bond Rose Garden, and the Winter Garden, which provides longed-for colors in the grey of winter. For details, call (610) 328–8025.

MERION

The art lovers in our family have always been awe-struck by the paintings at the **Barnes Foundation** on Latches Lane, one of the nation's most amazing private collections of Impressionist and Post-Impressionist art. This collection remained one of the art world's best-kept secrets until a recent national tour took many of its masterpieces to several major museums.

Dr. Albert C. Barnes was a businessman by vocation but art was his great love and he held very definite opinions about it. He collected over 180 Reniors, seventy Cézannes, and many Matisses—including a mural specifically commissioned for his home. His walls are cluttered with the works of Manet, Van Gogh, Picasso, and Seurat hanging beside those of Titian and El Greco, interspersed with wrought-iron hinges and latches, African masks, and antiques. Every piece has its place, and Dr. Barnes chose that place for a reason.

The Barnes Foundation recently re-opened after the tour and a restoration project. Call (610) 664–0290 for days and hours.

GLENSIDE

The **Keswick Theater,** Easton Road and Keswick Avenue, offers children's theater productions from time to time. Call for information: (215) 572–7650.

FORT WASHINGTON

There are no "no-no's" at the **Childventure Museum,** a hands-on, imaginative learning environment aimed at kids ten and under. When Faith's kids were preschoolers, they loved playing on the safe, indoor climbing structures, and trying on dress-up costumes in the Storybook Room, where everything is scaled down to fit younger children. The museum is in the Fort Washington Office Campus, at 430 Virginia Drive; telephone (215) 643–9906.

SOUTHAMPTON/CHURCHVILLE

Trails at the **Churchville Nature Center,** 501 Churchville Lane, are open from sun-up to sun-down daily. Inside the Nature Center, you can view dioramas depicting local wildlife. There are also children's programs, such as nature crafts, junior naturalist hikes, and activities centered on the Lenape Native Americans. The Center is open Tuesday through Sunday, 9:00 A.M. to 5:00 P.M.; call (215) 357–4005 for more information.

LANGHORNE

On "Sky Splash," kids and their parents share an oversized raft as an 8-foot rubber duckie douses them all with cool water. At another point, a huge shower head sprays the whole family at once. At **Sesame Place,** the whole idea is "intergenerational play." That's why many of the water rides use rafts that hold two or even six people. The outdoor play activities are designed for all ages. We've found that even kids too grown up for Cookie Monster can't help but enjoy many of the water rides and physical play environments.

You can walk down "Sesame Street," a full-size replica of the thoroughfare seen on the popular TV show, and take pictures of your kids in front of Bert and Ernie's house. At "Sesame Studio," kids can actually be a part of "The Amazing Adventures of Elmo and Zoe," and participate in science exhibits and special effects. There are over fifty kid-powered physical play elements such as "Nets and Climbs" and "Ernie's Bed Bounce."

The *New York Times* recently included Sesame Place on its list of best water parks in the United States. The park has thirteen water attractions, and most will appeal to all members of your family. "Big Bird's Rambling River" is a winding, relaxing circular tube ride our kids can go around and around all

At Sesame Place, outdoor play activities like this giant Marble Bag are designed for all ages.
(Courtesy Sesame Place)

afternoon. Even very young children have no fear on "Teeny Tiny Tidal Waves" and the "Rubber Duckie Pond."

Every day you can see a parade or a show starring Sesame Street characters, or just "bump into" a Twiddlebug walking down the street.

Sesame Place is located in Langhorne about thirty minutes from Philadelphia at Exit 29A on I–95 North. Operating days and hours vary, with the park opening in May for weekends only; starting in mid-May daily 10:00 A.M. to 5:00 P.M.; staying open later after Memorial Day and returning to weekend-only hours after Labor Day until mid-October when it closes for the season. For hours, call (215) 752–7070. Regular admission (ages three to fifty-four) costs $21.95; seniors, $18.95; children two and under are free. Discounts are available for families of four or more, or during late-afternoon hours. Most areas are accessible to the disabled, and special events include some designed for disabled children. Bathing suits are required for all water attractions.

FALLSINGTON

When he was living at Pennsbury Manor, William Penn attended Quaker

Meeting at Falls Meeting in Fallsington, a town built around its meeting-houses. Guided tours start at the **Gillingham Store** and include several restored historic buildings: **Moon-Williamson House; Burges-Lippincott House;** and the **Stage Coach Tavern.** Fallsington is located on Route 13 off I–95. For details, contact Historic Fallsington, Inc.; at (215) 295–6567.

MORRISVILLE

Pennsylvania was William Penn's "holy experiment," a colony founded on Quaker moral principles. Although he lived here for a total of about four years, **Pennsbury Manor** was never far from his thoughts. Today his home has been restored, complete with icehouse, stable, smokehouse, garden, and livestock. The boathouse contains a replica of the vessel Penn used to commute to Philadelphia. The oven in the bake and brew house can bake up to thirty loaves of bread at a time.

On Sunday afternoons from April to October, Pennsbury Manor offers living history just for families. The Visitor Center has an activity room where kids can try seventeenth-century skills, such as writing with a quill pen, or seventeenth-century games. Geese, peacocks, sheep, and a donkey—authentic breeds wherever possible—populate the farm.

Pennsbury Manor is located at 400 Pennsbury Memorial Road in Morrisville, and is open Tuesday through Saturday 9:00 A.M. to 5:00 P.M. and Sunday from noon to 5:00 P.M. Call (215) 946–0400 for information.

WASHINGTON CROSSING

We picture "Washington's crossing" as in the famous painting, with George Washington standing heroically in the small boat as his troops row across the Delaware to surprise the Hessians on Christmas Day.

The German artist had never seen Washington's Crossing when he painted it in the nineteenth century. It may not be safe to stand up in a small boat, but the image depicts an artist's impression of a historic event. (It is owned by the Washington's Crossing Foundation.) In the Memorial Building at **Washington Crossing Historic Park,** you can see a copy of the painting by Emanuel Leutz—and it's larger than life in more ways than one. (The painting is 20 feet long, 12 feet tall.)

A thirty-minute film at the Visitor Center describes the events of December 25, 1776. Washington planned his surprise attack from his headquarters in the **Thompson-Neely House,** and he ate dinner before the crossing at the **Old Ferry Inn.** In the **Durham Boat House** you can see the boats actually used for the crossing.

Every year on Christmas Day, the park hosts a re-enactment of Washington's crossing. Other special events here include Gingerbread Days, Tavern Nights, and special activities in honor of Washington's birthday. "Gazebo Games," another special event, lets kids try out the games and toys enjoyed by eighteenth-century children.

Bowman's Hill Tower and **Bowman's Hill Wildflower Preserve** (215–862–2924 or 862–3166) are both located on the grounds of Washington Crossing Historic Park. During the Revolution, sentries were posted in Bowman's Hill Tower, which has now been restored. Surrounding the tower you'll see breath-taking varieties of wildflowers. You can pick up a self-guided tour map that also includes a list of flowers currently in bloom.

The Visitor Center and historic buildings are open Monday through Saturday 9:00 A.M. to 5:00 P.M. and on Sunday from noon to 5:00 P.M. There is a fee for the buildings. The park grounds, however, are open at no charge from 8:00 A.M. until sunset. For information, call (215) 493–4076.

NEW HOPE

In the summer the streets of New Hope bustle with people drawn to the over 200 art galleries, craft shops, restaurants, and history this town offers. But New Hope welcomes visitors any time of the year. You can get more information about New Hope by contacting the New Hope Information Center, 1 West Mechanic Street, New Hope 18938 (215–862–5880) or Village of New Hope, Greater New Hope Chamber of Commerce, P.O. Box 633, New Hope 18938 (215–862–3730).

If you wish to take any kind of ride or tour, including walking tours, check at **Gerenser's Exotic Ice Cream** at 22 South Main Street, where tickets and schedules are available. For example, you can purchase tickets for a colonial walking tour (215–862–2050). This is also where you get tickets for Coryell's Ferry (see below). Have some ice cream while you're here! To find out about "Ghost Tours," call (215) 357–5637 or (215) 957–9988.

Artists began settling in New Hope in the late 1800s, but the town started out as **Coryell's Ferry,** which started carrying passengers across the Delaware in canoes in 1733. Ferries still operate here for half-hour tours, only now they use more commodious paddleboats. Ferries leave Coryell's Ferry at Gerenser's Exotic Ice Cream, 22 South Main Street, April through October starting at noon. Call (215) 862–2050 for details or to find out about special kids' days on the ferry.

The Delaware Canal became operational in 1840 and, at its height, mules hauled thousands of barges on the canal carrying loads of coal and limestone. The canal includes twenty-five lift locks, nine aqueducts, and 106 bridges. You can take a ride on one of these barges, sailing past eighteenth-century homes, gardens, and workshops, any day from May to October, at 11:30 A.M., 1:00 P.M., 2:00 P.M., 3:00 P.M., 4:30 P.M. and 7:00 P.M. In April and November, trips are offered only on Wednesdays, Saturdays, and Sundays and the 7:00 P.M. trip is omitted. For a current schedule, contact **New Hope Mule Barge** on New Street by calling (215) 862–2842. Another boat ride is available through **Boat Rides at Wells Ferry** at the end of Ferry Steet on River Road (215–862–5965).

We especially enjoy just strolling along the canal, watching the barges go by. Some of the restaurants here have views of the canal.

The **New Hope and Ivyland Railroad,** built in 1889, eventually made the canal obsolete. You can board the train at Bridge and Stockton streets. If you take this train on its 9-mile narrated trip to Lahaska, you will notice a curved trestle bridge. If this bridge looks like something right out of *The Perils of Pauline,* that's because this actually was the bridge they used in those movies. Trains run daily from April to November, weekends only from January until March. In December, special Santa Claus rides are offered. Tickets are $7.50 for adults, $5.95 for seniors, $3.95 for kids three to eleven, and $1.00 for children under three. Call (215) 862–2332 for details.

LAHASKA

In **Peddler's Village,** outside New Hope on routes 202 and 263, you'll discover a museum to charm anyone who has ever stood spellbound watching a merry-go-round. Charlotte Dinger's outstanding collection of antique carousel horses and related art is now exhibited in a new museum, **Carousel World** (215–794–8960). The centerpiece is a working carousel with two chariots and forty-eight beautifully carved animals—including two polar bears. While in Peddler's Village, take a look at some of the unusual shops here.

POINT PLEASANT

The signers of the Declaration of Independence had to sweat it out in the notorious Philadelphia humidity, but you don't have to. Point Pleasant, north of Lahaska and New Hope, offers some great ways to cool off in its inviting, kid-friendly rapids. Several outfitters rent canoes, tubes, and rafts from April through October. To make reservations (which are required) or to find out about prices and special Pedal and Paddle trips, call **Bucks County River Country** (215–297–8400) or **Point Pleasant Canoe and Tube, Inc.** (215–297–8406).

DOYLESTOWN

On Pine Street in the charming town of Doylestown, with its cast-iron lamp-posts and neat nineteenth-century houses, stands what can only be described as a castle, not of stone but of poured concrete, brainchild of Henry Chapman Mercer (1856–1930).

In 1916, Mercer built what is now the **Mercer Museum** (84 South Pine Street near Ashland) with its turrets and parapets, to house his collection of over 50,000 artifacts and tools of over sixty different American trades. Entering the central court of the museum, you find yourself surrounded by odds and ends hanging over your head: a Conestoga wagon; a whaling skiff; wooden buckets. Then, take the elevator up to the top floor and walk down, working your way through the implements left behind by shoemakers, bakers, candle-makers, milliners, and farmers of America's past.

Our kids felt that the highlight of the collection was the vampire-killing kit. They also enjoyed hunting for the footprints left in the concrete by Mercer's pet dog. The museum is unheated, so bring your sweater. The museum is open Monday through Saturday 10:00 A.M. to 5:00 P.M., Sunday noon to 5:00 P.M. On Tuesdays, the museum closes at 9:00 P.M. There are special children's pro-grams, as well as FolkFest in May. Call (215) 345–0210 for details.

Across the street from the Mercer Museum, the **James A. Michener Museum** (138 South Pine Street; (215–340–9800) is a good art collection par-tially housed in the former Bucks County Jail. The novelist James Michener was born and raised in Doylestown and was closely involved with the muse-um since its inception. Scheduled to open soon is the Mari Sabusawa Michener Wing's family education center, which will feature books, videos, and children's learning tools.

Also within walking distance is the **County Theater,** showing art and vintage, as well as first-run, movies; the picturesque **Doylestown Inn;** as well as many other restaurants and shops.

The **Moravian Pottery and Tile Works,** the legacy of Mercer's effort to preserve an American craft, is also nearby. You can purchase Moravian tiles here. Mercer's home, **Fonthill,** has forty-four rooms, eighteen fireplaces and thirty-two staircases, and is open to visitors (reservations are recommended). Both Fonthill and the Moravian Tile Works are located on East Court Street. Call (215) 348–9461 for information.

Gardeners get a breath of fresh air at **Henry Schmieder Arboretum of Delaware Valley College** (on Route 202, (215–345–1500) and the nearby **Inn at Fordhook Farm** (a bed and breakfast, call 215–345–1766). The Burpee Family (of Burpee Seeds) developed many well-known seed varieties in this area.

Another fun idea: Try ballooning. For information, call **Color the Sky, Inc.** at (215) 340–9966.

CHALFONT

Children's eyes grow wide when they see this tiny landscape filled with doll-like figures, each one unique, each one singing a Christmas carol. At **Byers' Choice Ltd.** (4355 County Line Road; 215–822–6700), the Byers family and their employees hand-sculpt thousands of delightful Caroler figurines every year, giving a percentage of their profits to charity. They invite visitors to watch the delicate faces molded and painted, and to tour their gallery of little carolers in various costumes and settings. The factory is open at no charge Monday through Saturday, 10:00 A.M. to 4:00 P.M. Understandably, it is closed January (to recover) and major holidays.

PIPERSVILLE

Ballooning adventures are available here by contacting **Keystone State Balloon Tours, Inc.,** P.O. Box 162, Pipersville 18947; (610) 294–8034.

PLUMSTEADVILLE

At **Malmark, Inc. Bellcraftsmen** (Bell Crest Park, Route 611), the world's largest manufacturer of tuned handbells offers tours of their factory by appointment only. Call (215) 766–7200 for an appointment.

HILLTOWN

Perhaps you or your kids have read *The Good Earth* or other books by Pearl S. Buck. The author settled in the 1835 farmhouse at **Green Hills Farm.** In her office here she wrote more than one hundred novels. Buck is admired not only for her writing but for her work to help Amerasian children through the Pearl S. Buck Foundation, which still has offices at the Farm. The home is filled with Chinese art, including a 500-year-old Buddha, and a wall hanging that was a gift from the Dalai Lama. Guided tours are available March through December, Tuesday through Saturday, at 10:30 A.M., 1:30 P.M., and 2:30 P.M. On Sundays, tours leave at 1:30 P.M. and 2:30 P.M. only. The house is located in Hilltown, at 520 Dublin Road. Call (215) 249–0100 for more information.

WORCESTER

The historians at **Peter Wentz Farmstead** have done an exceptional job researching and restoring this farm to its appearance in 1777. If you thought colonial farms were painted in subdued tones, you'll be amazed at the paint colors and wild patterns on the walls: dots, zig-zags, stripes, and more.

Come on a Saturday afternoon and you can watch staff members demonstrate colonial crafts using authentic techniques. You can watch spinning, weaving, candle-making, and cooking, as well as unusual arts such as *scheren-schnitte,* the German art of paper-cutting.

The farmstead is located just off Route 73 at Schultz Road. It is open year-round Tuesday to Saturday 10 A.M. to 4:00 P.M., and Sunday 1:00 to 4:00 P.M.; closed Mondays, Thanksgiving, and Christmas. Donations are accepted. For details, call (610) 584–5104.

Only a few blocks away, on Weikel Road, you can see the **Morgan Log House,** built in 1695 and over 90 percent intact. The Morgans, who lived here, had ten children, one of whom grew up to become the mother of Daniel Boone. Open April to November weekends only, noon to 5:00 P.M., or by appointment. Call (610) 368–2480.

SKIPPACK

Come to **Skippack Village** to shop in the country-style crafts shops and boutiques. The village attracts many visitors around the holidays when you can walk the streets by the light of luminaria. Also on Route 73 is the **Ironmaster's House and Museum** (610–584–4441).

SCHWENKSVILLE

Seven miles down Skippack Pike (Route 73) from the Peter Wentz Farmstead, you can see an excellent example of Colonial Revival architecture. **Pennypacker Mills** (Route 73 and Haldeman Road; 610–287–9349) was owned by the Pennypacker family as early as 1747. In 1900, Samuel W. Pennypacker purchased it and restored it in colonial style. Pennypacker was governor of Pennsylvania from 1903 to 1907, as well as a respected historian, collector, and farmer. The home is surrounded by fifteen acres of gardens landscaped in the English "natural" style. Today the site is preserved by Montgomery County as a turn-of-the-century country gentleman's estate.

Pennypacker Mills hosts special events for children, including a Halloween celebration with horse-drawn hay rides. For Earth Day, a family event is coordinated with the Perkiomen Valley Watershed Association. Special children's events re-create the neighborhood parties once held by the Pennypacker daughters. There are also living history events and Christmas holiday celebrations. Call for details about these events and others for adults, families, and young children.

Pennypacker Mills is open free of charge Tuesday through Saturday, 10:00 A.M. to 4:00 P.M., and on Sunday from 1:00 to 4:00 P.M. It is closed Monday and major holidays.

Also in Schwenksville, the **Philadelphia Folk Festival** brings music, crafts, fun, and thousands of people to Old Pool Farm every August. For information, call (800) 556–FOLK.

ALBURTIS

The anthracite iron industry played an important role in the development of this area, beginning in 1839. **Lock Ridge Furnace Museum** on Franklin Street in Alburtis (610–435–4664) operated as a furnace until 1914, and is now one of the sites administered by the Lehigh County Historical Society. The museum and furnace are open May through September, weekdays 1:00 to 4:00 P.M.

MOUNT BETHEL

The area from Slateford to Wind Gap was once known as the Slate Belt, because of the large amount of slate produced here. The **Slate Belt Historical Museum,** housed in a lovely old church on Route 611 in Mount Bethel, tells the history of this area, which also produced tobacco. You can see a replica of a slate shanty, a printing press, farm tools and implements, and Native American relics. The museum is open weekends from May through September, and hosts special events such as a very popular craft show. Call (717) 897–6862 for details.

ALLENTOWN

Allentown is home to one of the best traditional amusement parks in the country, plus one of its best water parks, as well as a kid-friendly art museum, a gristmill, and the Museum of Indian Culture.

Most museums look at our nation's history through the eyes of Europeans. The **Museum of Indian Culture and Lenni Lenape Historical Society** takes a different viewpoint. Children will enjoy the many hands-on exhibits that illuminate Native American culture, as well as the exhibits of tools, baskets, and crafts. Three ceremonies are held annually: Corn Planting in May; Roasting Ears of Corn in August; and Time of Thanksgiving in October. There are also picnic facilities, two nature trails, and a fish hatchery.

The museum is located on Fish Hatchery Road. It is open Tuesday through Sunday, noon to 3:00 P.M. Admission is $2.00; students and seniors $1.50; special group rates are available. Wheelchair accessible. Call (610) 797–2121 for details.

The Junior Gallery at the **Allentown Art Museum** at Fifth and Court streets offers hands-on art activities and touchable sculpture for children. The museum is open Tuesday through Saturday 10:00 A.M. to 5:00 P.M. and Sundays noon until 5:00 P.M. Admission is $3.50 for adults, $3.00 for seniors, $2.00 for students, and free for kids under twelve. The museum also shows family-oriented films. For information, call (610) 432–4333.

Haines Mill, 3600 Haines Mill Road, was built in 1760 and operated until 1956, after having been renovated in 1909 with a water turbine power source. It is open weekends from May until September, 1:00 to 4:00 P.M. Call (610) 435–4664.

Housed in Allentown's Old Courthouse at 5th and Hamilton streets, the **Lehigh County Historical Museum** displays artifacts from the earliest inhabitants of the Lehigh Valley, the Lenni Lenape, as well as from the Pennsylvania Germans and other settlers who came to this area. The museum also includes the Scott Andrew Trexler II Memorial Library, an extensive collection of county and genealogical records. The museum and library are open 10:00 A.M. to 4:00 P.M., Monday through Saturday. The museum is also open Sunday 1:00 to 4:00 P.M. Call (610) 435–4664 for details.

Did you know that during the Revolutionary War, when the British occupied Philadelphia, all the bells in the city were removed so that the British would not be able to melt them down for ammunition? From September 1777 to June 1778, the Liberty Bell was hidden under the floor of Allentown's Zion Church at 622 Hamilton Mall, 1 block away from the Lehigh County Historical Museum. Today, the **Liberty Bell Shrine** includes an exact replica of the famous bell, as well as flags, maps, weapons, uniforms, and a 46-foot mural showing scenes from the Revolution. Open Monday through Saturday, noon to 4:00 P.M., and on Sundays from 2:00 to 4:00 P.M. Admission is free. Call (610) 435–4232 for information.

The Lehigh County Historical Society administers a number of sites, including several historic homes. **Trout Hall** (414 Walnut Street; 610–435–4664) is Allentown's oldest home, built in 1770 by the son of the city's founder, William Allen. The **Troxell-Steckel House** in nearby Egypt (4229 Reliance Street; 610–435–4664) is an excellent example of a rural German-style farmhouse. Its barn contains a collection of old buggies and wagons. Trout Hall is open April through November, Tuesday through Saturday, noon to 3:00 P.M. and on Sunday from 1:00 to 4:00 P.M. The Troxell-Steckel House is open weekends only 1:00 to 4:00 P.M.

Frank Buchman, founder of the world-wide Moral Re-armament Movement, who was nominated for two Nobel Prizes, lived at 117 North 11th Street in Allentown. The **Frank Buchman House** displays some of Buchman's

EMILY AND FAITH'S FAVORITE EVENTS IN THE PHILADELPHIA COUNTRYSIDE

Philadelphia Folk Festival (weekend before Labor Day)
(215) 242–0150, (215) 247–1300 or (800) 556–FOLK
Scarecrow Festival Weekend at Peddler's Village (215) 794–4000
Celebration of Lights, Core Creek Park (November to December)
(215) 757–0571
Great Allentown Fair (610) 433–7541 (office) (610) 435–7469
(show information) (late August)
Mercer Museum FolkFest (May) (215) 345–0210
Pennsylvania Fair, Bensalem and Philadelphia (mid-May)
(800) 749–247
Great Pumpkin Carve in Chadds Ford (October) (610) 338–7376
Devon Horse Show (ten days surrounding Memorial Day week-
end) (610) 964–0550
Time of Thanksgiving, Lenni Lenape Museum (autumn)
(610) 797–2121
Longwood Gardens Christmas Display (November to January 1)
(610) 388–6741

souvenirs from an extraordinary life. The house is open for tours weekends only 1:00 to 4:00 P.M.

When it's time for a change of pace, head out of downtown Allentown to **Dorney Park and Wildwater Kingdom.** Among other rides and attractions, Dorney Park has three world-class roller coasters, and Wildwater Kingdom has eleven water slides. Younger children will love meeting the Berenstain Bears, playing in the TotSpot, and cooling off in two water park areas specifically for small fry. Our kids could have spent the whole day in the giant wave pool.

Dorney Park and Wildwater Kingdom is located near Exit 16 on Route 309 South, at 3700 Hamilton Boulevard. Hours for both parks vary according to season. Dorney Park is open weekends only in May and September, then daily from Memorial Day to Labor Day. Wildwater Kingdom is open mid-May to Labor Day, and selected weekends in September. Tickets cost $24.95 for anyone 48 inches or taller, $4.95 for anyone under 47 inches and seniors, and are free for children under three. These prices include admission to both parks. For more information call (610) 395–3724.

If your kids are fascinated by crystal formations, rocks, minerals, and stalagmites and stalactites, don't miss **Lost River Caverns,** located in nearby Hellertown (call 610–838–8767).

Other attractions in the Allentown are include **Trexler-Lehigh County Game Preserve** (5150 Game Preserve Road in Schnecksville; 610–799–4171) and the **Great Allentown Fair** (302 North 17th Street; 610–435–SHOW).

CLAUSSVILLE

Children can picture what school must have been like in the **Claussville One-Room Schoolhouse,** in which children learned from 1893 until 1956. They can imagine kids sitting at these very desks, reading the very books displayed there. The schoolhouse, one of the Lehigh County Historical Society sites, is located on Route 100 in Claussville, and is open on weekends from May through September, 1:00 P.M. to 4:00 P.M. Call (610) 435–4664.

BETHLEHEM

The Star of Bethlehem shines on Star Mountain every night of the year, watching over this city founded by Moravian settlers and named "Bethlehem" on Christmas Eve, 1741. You may wish to visit during Christkindlmarkt in December when lanterns are lit, or in August when Musikfest is held. But no matter when you visit, start out at the Visitor Center, where you can see a film and multimedia presentation about the city. You can pick up a schedule of events and walking tour map, or schedule a guided tour. The Visitor Center is in the Historic Area, off Route 378, at 52 West Broad Street. Call (610) 868–1513, 867–0173, or (800) 360–8687.

Don't miss **Gemein Haus** at 66 West Church Street, a log cabin five stories tall, built entirely without nails. When the Moravians first came to Bethlehem, this was their church, their sleeping quarters, and their workshop. Now it serves as a museum of Moravian history, exhibiting Moravian furniture, needlework, toys, and art. Open Tuesday through Saturday, 1:00 to 4:00 P.M. Like most attractions in Bethlehem, it is closed in January.

From there, visit Bethlehem's **18th Century Industrial Quarter** on Old York Road, (610–691–0603). There is a self-guided walking tour of the quarter. Pick up a walking tour brochure at the Luckenback Mill. Groups can call ahead to arrange a tour of the buildings.

NAZARETH

Like Bethlehem, **Nazareth** was founded in the 1700s by Moravian settlers. Today, Nazareth is also the home of Martin Guitars. The **Nazareth Area Visitors Center** (610–759–9174) is housed in the **Martin Family Homestead** at 201 North Main Street next to the old Martin Guitar factory. The current **Martin Guitar Factory** is at 510 Sycamore Street, and offers free guided tours Monday through Friday at 1:15 P.M. For groups of ten or more, reservations are required and a $2.00 fee per person is charged. Call (610) 759–2837 for further details.

Other sites in Nazareth include **Moravian Historical Society and Whitefield** (pronounced WIT-field) **House Museum** (214 East Center Street; 610–759–5070) and **Nazareth Speedway** (located on Highway 191 in Nazareth, call 610–759–8000 for tickets).

EASTON

Generations of kids can recognize the distinctive packaging of Crayola crayons. Due to re-open in Spring 1996, with a new Visitor Center in downtown Easton, Crayola tours will allow kids to learn how Crayola crayons are made. For information, contact **Binney & Smith Crayola Factory** by calling (800) CRAYOLA.

The Delaware Canal runs from Easton to Bristol, and its area has recently become a National Heritage Corridor. There are opportunities to learn about the canal's place in history in Bristol, New Hope,x and other towns. Check out the **Canal Boat Ride** off South 25th Street (610–250–6700) and the **Canal Museum** on Route 611 South (610–250–6700).

BREINIGSVILLE

Terry Hill Waterpark, located on Route 222 in Breinigsville, has three pools, nine water slides, a kiddie area, refreshments, and more. The water park is open noon to 6:00 P.M. daily beginning in June. In July and August, it's open noon to 7:00 P.M. weekdays and noon to 8:00 P.M. weekends. Admission is $12.50 for those under 48 inches tall, and $15.00 for all others. Call (610) 395–0222 for details.

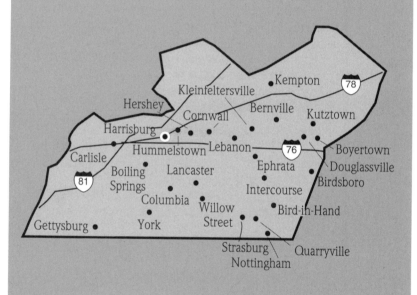

Kempton

Kleinfeltersville

78

Hershey
Cornwall
Bernville
Kutztown

Harrisburg

Lebanon
76
Boyertown

Carlisle
Hummelstown
Douglassville

81
Boiling
Springs
Lancaster
Ephrata
Birdsboro

Intercourse

Columbia
Willow
Street
Bird-in-Hand

Gettysburg
York
Strasburg
Quarryville
Nottingham

Hershey–Pennsylvania
Dutch Country

HERSHEY–PENNSYLVANIA DUTCH COUNTRY

H ershey–Pennsylvania Dutch Country beckons with amusement parks, historical sites, Pennsylvania Dutch arts and crafts, and lots of train rides. This is the Keystone State's classic countryside, with Amish farms and roadside markets. It was also the site of the Battle of Gettysburg, where more American lives were lost than in any other single battle in U.S. history.

Harrisburg, the state capital on the shores of the Susquehanna, is in the midst of a renaissance under its active mayor, Steven Reed. City Island, once abandoned, has been transformed into a family entertainment spot, with miniature golf, the *Pride of the Susquehanna* riverboat, Class AA baseball, a children's railroad, and more.

Kids delight in Hershey, ChocolateTown USA, with its street lights shaped like chocolate kisses and its triple helping of kid-friendly attractions— Hersheypark, ZooAmerica, and Chocolate World.

While you're planning your trip, you can use the Internet to "Ask the Amish" about their customs and culture. The Pennsylvania Dutch Country Information Center site on the World Wide Web can be accessed at http://padutch.welcome.com. One thing you'll learn online is that the Amish appreciate it when tourists respect their need for privacy and their dislike of cameras. The home page even allows your kids to "blow the whistle" on the Strasburg Railroad.

Families who visit Pennsylvania Dutch Country often comment on the food: it's abundant and inexpensive. Family-style restaurants abound, with diners seated at large tables and delicious, simple food passed around in large bowls.

The Pennsylvania Dutch area is a great place for a farm vacation. For more information on a vacation of any type in Pennsylvania Dutch country, call the Pennsylvania Dutch Convention and Visitors Bureau at (717) 299–8901. To learn about farm vacations, write to the Pennsylvania Farm Vacation Association, Pennsylvania Department of Agriculture, Marketing Department, 2301 North Cameron Street, Harrisburg 17110–9408.

KEMPTON

The **Hawk Mountain Sanctuary** attracts bird watchers from up and down the East Coast to Berks County to watch the many varieties of hawks and bald eagles that pass through the area on their annual migrations. There are hiking trails of varying degrees of difficulty and one lookout area that is accessible to the handicapped. The Visitor Center is open daily year-round. Admission is $4.00 for adults, $2.00 for children six to twelve. Bring binoculars, wear a jacket, and, to find out what kinds of birds of prey can currently be seen. The Hawk Mountain Sanctuary is located several miles east of Route 61, and several miles north of I–78, near the town of Kempton. Call (610) 756–6961 for more information.

The **Hawk Mountain Line** gives families the choice of a ride on a trolley or a steam train—a tough choice for many kids. The steam train ride is about 6 miles round-trip and takes about forty minutes. The 9-mile trolley route runs about thirty-five minutes. Pack a picnic and have the train drop you off at a trackside grove. The steam train runs on Sunday from May through October and Saturday during July, August, and October. The trolley runs Saturday during June and September. Tours leave every hour on the hour, 1:00 to 4:00 P.M. Fares are $4.00 for adults, $2.00 for children ages two to eleven.

Annual special events include a Kid's Fun Weekend, Halloween Train, and Santa Claus Special. Call for schedules and more information: (610) 756–6469.

KUTZTOWN

Just use your imagination and you can see the ice cream cone, the crystal ballroom, the giant's tooth, and the prairie dogs inside the geological formations at **Crystal Cave,** Kutztown, between Allentown and Reading. After your underground adventure, try some of the free activities such as the nature trail, picnic area, playground, and Amish buggy rides. Crystal Cave is open every day from March through November. For information and the schedule of guided tours, call (610) 683–6765.

Little kids who love swords and shields, daggers, maces, and armor will enjoy the displays at the **Cut and Thrust Edged Weapons Museum** (211–213 West Main Street in Kutztown). Admission is $3.00. Hours are subject to seasonal change, so call (610) 683–5683 for information.

BOYERTOWN

You may not know about the role this region played in the early automobile industry, but you'll learn about this and more at the **Boyertown Museum of Historic Vehicles.** The museum, open 9:30 A.M. to 4:30 P.M. daily except Mondays, displays over seventy-five vehicles including a 1907 Duryea Buggynaut. It is located at 28 Warwick Street in Boyertown and is open Tuesday through Friday 9:00 A.M. to 4:00 P.M., Saturday and Sunday 9:30 A.M. to 4:00 P.M. Call (610) 367–2090.

DOUGLASSVILLE

Together, the **Mary Merritt Doll Museum** and **Merritt's Museum of Early Childhood** in Douglassville will delight any child. At the Doll Museum your children can see literally thousands of antique dolls, the oldest dating from the 1660s. Over fifty doll houses are on display. Just stroll around the toy trains, toy boats, rag dolls, pull toys, baby dolls, hobby horses, and paper dolls. We recommend parents consider their children's maturity level; very little children will be frustrated that they can't touch.

The Museum of Early Childhood was designed to give other family members something to do while the doll enthusiasts were in the Doll Museum. It includes Colonial and Victorian antiques and Native American relics. Admission is $3.00 for adults, $1.50 for children five to twelve.

The Merritt Museums are located between Pottstown and Reading on Route 422. They are both open Monday through Saturday 10:00 A.M. to 5:00 P.M.; Sundays and holidays 1:00 to 5:00 P.M. One admission ticket gets you into both museums. Call (610) 385–3809 for the Doll Museum and (610) 385–3408 for the Museum of Early Childhood. Each museum has its own gift shop.

BIRDSBORO

Daniel Boone was born and grew up in a log cabin at **Daniel Boone Homestead,** 400 Daniel Boone Road (610–582–4900). Here you can see a working blacksmith's shop, smokehouse, bake oven, and sawmill. Call (610) 582–4900 for information about tours, picnicking, camping, and the game sanctuary.

BERNVILLE

Koziar's Christmas Village, 782 Christmas Village Road, is in Bernville, off Route 183. More than 500,000 lights sparkle on the lake-side house, along with its walkways, trees, and ten outbuildings including Santa's post office and toy shop. Open evenings only from October through New Year's Day. Call (610) 488–1110 for hours and days, which vary seasonally. There is an admission charge.

KLEINFELTERSVILLE

Bundle up, bring your binoculars, and come to the **Middle Creek Wildlife Management Area** in January or February and you can see literally thousands of tundra swans! In spring and fall there are many other species of migrating waterfowl. There are also hiking trails, including one specially marked for the visually impaired, plus fishing and hunting in designated areas only, including one trout stream that's accessible to the disabled. Call the Visitor Center at (717) 733–1512. Picnic areas are available, but you must not feed the birds.

LEBANON

This is the one town where you can see how genuine Lebanon bologna is made. The Daniel Weaver Company, which produces both Weaver's famous Lebanon Bologna and Baum's Bologna, is the oldest commercial manufacturer of Lebanon bologna in the United States. Here you can see the outdoor smokehouses, visit exhibits, enjoy free samples, and visit their retail store. The Weaver Company is open Monday through Saturday 9:00 A.M. to 4:00 P.M., free of charge. Free tours are available. For more information call (717) 274–6100 or (800) WEAVERS.

And speaking of food factory tours, you can actually twist your own pretzel at the first pretzel bakery in the country, **Julius Sturgis Pretzel House** (219 East Main Street in nearby Lititz; 717–626–4354).

CORNWALL

The most important difference between **Cornwall Iron Furnace** and Hopewell Furnace (see "Philadelphia Countryside") is that most of Cornwall is original, while Hopewell is reconstructed. Cornwall Iron Furnace operated from the 1740s until the 1880s. A guide takes you through the ironmaking complex, pointing out the 32-foot-tall furnace itself. The furnace is open daily Tuesday through Saturday 9:00 A.M. to 5:00 P.M., Sunday noon to 5:00 P.M. It is open Memorial Day, Independence Day, and Labor Day. Admission is charged. Call (717) 272–9711 for information.

Mount Hope Estate and Winery, an attractive Victorian estate, hosts wine-tastings daily. In addition, if you visit at the right time, you may enjoy one of several unusual seasonal events. On weekends from August through mid-October join the raucous revelry of the Pennsylvania Renaissance Faire. Meet sixteenth-century knaves and wenches, jesters, pirates, princesses, and knights who will immerse your family in a spectacle of living theater. Events include jousting, human chess, children's games, crafts, short plays such as *Robin Hood,* and dancing. In late October Mount Hope is host to "An Evening of Classic Horror" and from the end of October through mid-

Queen Elizabeth I presides over revelries such as jousting, human chess, games, plays, and dancing at the Pennsylvania Renaissance Faire. (Courtesy Pennsylvania Renaissance Faire)

November, you can be mystified at "Edgar Allen Poe Evermore." From Thanksgiving weekend until after Christmas, the estate is decked out quite differently for a festive "Charles Dickens Victorian Christmas." Call (717) 665–7021 for details on schedules and admission.

Easily accessible to Mt. Hope on the opposite side of Route 340, you'll find **Plain & Fancy Farm** with its buggy rides and Pennsylvania Dutch crafts and food (see also page 51).

EPHRATA

Older children may be interested in learning about a true alternative life style once practiced at **Ephrata Cloister** (632 West Main Street; 717–733–6600). Here you can step into another reality in twelve restored buildings where hymns still seem to echo. Open Monday to Saturday 9:00 A.M. to 5:00 P.M. and Sunday from noon to 5:00 P.M. Ephrata is also an interesting town where you may wish to browse in the art galleries and craft shops. Stop by at **Artworks at Doneckers,** 100 North State Street (717–738–9503).

INTERCOURSE

Kids have lots of questions about the Pennsylvania Dutch. What's it like to dress in Amish clothes? How does it feel to ride in an Amish buggy? And deeper questions: What do the Amish believe? Why do they live differently from most of us? Their questions will be answered at the **People's Place** on Main Street in Intercourse (717–768–7171).

After viewing the twenty-five-minute film, kids in first through eighth grade can actually try school lessons used by Amish children their age. They can also learn to work the signal indicators on an Amish carriage. Hands-on exhibits and a collection of folk art help build an understanding of the life style chosen by the Amish and Mennonites. Open Monday through Saturday, 9:30 A.M. to 9:30 P.M. Memorial Day through Labor Day. Off-season the museum is open 9:30 A.M. to 5:30 P.M. The **People's Place Quilt Museum** is adjacent and can be reached at (717) 768–7101.

Behind People's Place you'll find the collection of over thirty craft shops called **Kitchen Kettle Village** (800–732–3530). You can see fudge being made and Shaker-style furniture being built.

BIRD-IN-HAND

Class is in session, with animated figures of a teacher and pupils in the **Weavertown One Room Schoolhouse** on Route 340 east of Bird-in-Hand.

The building, desks, and blackboard are original. Open Good Friday through Thanksgiving, seven days a week, starting at 10:00 A.M. Closing time changes seasonally. Call (717) 768–3976 or 291–1888.

Lancaster County offers several opportunities to ride in a Pennsylvania Dutch buggy, but only one ride is owned and operated by an Amish family. You'll find it—**Aaron and Jessica's Buggy Rides**—at Plain & Fancy Farm on Route 340 between Bird-in-Hand and Intercourse. Also at Plain & Fancy, you can visit the **Amish Country Homestead** (3121 Old Philadelphia Pike in Bird-in-Hand; 717–392–8622).

You can also ride in an Amish carriage at **Abe's Buggy Rides** (717–392–1794), 2596 Old Philadelphia Pike in Bird-in-Hand. Open year-round, but closed on Sunday. For a tour of the area, contact **Amish Country Tours** (2323 Lincoln Highway East, Lancaster 17602; 717–393–2308 or 800–441–3505).

STRASBURG

Here, transportation enthusiasts can learn about toy trains, real trains, classic cars, and more.

It's almost overwhelming to walk into the huge collection of locomotives and rolling stock at the **Railroad Museum of Pennsylvania,** which specializes in railroad trains built or operated in Pennsylvania. Rolling Stock Hall is designed with a balcony and a pit so that you can see the twenty-four locomotives and passenger cars from different angles. Outdoors you can see some forty more cars. Open Monday through Saturday 9:00 A.M. to 5:00 P.M., Sunday noon to 5:00 P.M. Closed Mondays from November through April. Call (717) 687–8628.

After you've seen the Railroad Museum, cross the street for a forty-five-minute ride on the **Strasburg Railroad** (Route 741 East, 717–687–7522). Also within walking distance you'll find the **Choo Choo Barn** (717–687–7911), where fifteen miniature trains chug through 130 animated scenes. Open 10:00 A.M. to 5:00 P.M. daily, in summer 10:00 A.M. to 6:00 P.M. Strasburg Railroad admission is $7.00 for adults, $4.00 for children three to eleven.

You can also see model trains at the **National Toy Train Museum,** located at 300 Paradise Lane (717–687–8976), which is open April through October 10:00 A.M. to 5:00 P.M. In May, November, and December the museum is open weekends only. Admission to the National Toy Train Museum is $3.00 for adults, $1.50 for children five to twelve.

Fifty classic cars including several Tuckers (remember the movie *Tucker*?) are on display at the **Gast Classic Motorcars Exhibit** on Route 896. Open daily June through September 9:00 A.M. to 9:00 P.M. From October through May, the museum is open 9:00 A.M. to 9:00 P.M. on Friday and Saturday, but closes at 5:00 P.M. on Sunday through Thursday. Call (717) 687–9500. Admission to Gast Classic Motorcars is $6.00 for adults thirteen and above, $3.00 for children age seven to twelve.

You can even include horse-drawn vehicles by taking a ride at **Ed's Buggy Rides** (Route 896, 717–687–0360). A ride in a buggy costs $10.00 for adults, $5.00 for chidren six to twelve.

The old farmhouse at the **Amish Village** dates to 1840, and there's also a one-room school, windmill, blacksmith shop, and smokehouse. Forget your diet and indulge in Amish delights. The Village is located 2 miles north of Strasburg on Route 896 and is open daily from 9:00 A.M. to 5:00 P.M. in spring, summer, and fall. In the winter, the village is open 10:00 A.M. to 4:00 P.M. on weekends, weather permitting. Call (717) 687–8511 for details. Admission to the Amish Village is $5.50 for adults, $1.50 for children six to twelve.

See demonstrations of broom-making, candle-making, and quilting, visit an Amish school and grist mill, and take a ride on an Amish buggy at **Mill Bridge Village** on South Ronks Road, one-half mile south of Route 30 East. For information, call (800) MIL–BRIG.

QUARRYVILLE

Your kids have probably heard about Robert Fulton and his steamboat *Clermont,* nicknamed "Fulton's Folly." But few people realize how wide-ranging Fulton's interests were. Famous for his fine portraits, Fulton was also a respected scientist who patented many different devices. You can learn about this interesting man by visiting **Robert Fulton Birthplace** in Quarryville, north of Goshen on Route 222. Open Memorial Day to Labor Day, Saturday 11:00 A.M. to 4:00 P.M. and Sunday 1:00 to 5:00 P.M. Admission to Robert Fulton's birthplace is $1.00 for adults. Children twelve and under enter free. For information, call (717) 548–2679.

NOTTINGHAM

You can see how potato chips are made, and then try some chips still warm from the cooker at **Herr Foods, Inc.** The company offers free tours of its snack foods factory on routes 272 and 131 in Nottingham. Open Monday through Thursday 9:00 A.M. to 4:00 P.M., Friday 9:00 A.M. to noon. For details, call (800) 284–7488.

WILLOW STREET

The date "1719" appears on the door lintel of the **Hans Herr House,** 1849

Hans Herr Drive in Willow Street (717–464–4438). Check with the Visitor Center first for information about the home, garden, blacksmith's shop, and more. Open April through December, Monday through Saturday 9:00 A.M. to 4:00 P.M. Open by appointment only in the off-season. Admission to the Hans Herr House is $3.50 for adults, $1.00 for children ages seven to twelve. Call for information about special events such as the "Hans Herr Heritage Day" in August and the "Snitz Fest" (an apple festival) in October.

LANCASTER

Your six-year-old can drive an old-fashioned motorcar, your twelve-year-old can brave the Sky Princess roller coaster, your family can take a walk in the botanical gardens, and everyone can grab a carpet square and race down the giant slide. **Dutch Wonderland Family Fun Park** is located at 2249 Route 30 East in Lancaster (717–291–1888), next door to the Wax Museum of Lancaster County and within minutes of the Amish Farm and House, the Weavertown One-Room School, the Old Mill Stream Camping Manor, and a great deal of outlet shopping. Dutch Wonderland is open weekends in spring and fall, and daily from Memorial Day to Labor Day. Admission runs $12.00 to $17.00 for children over three and adults.

At the **Wax Museum of Lancaster County** (2249 Route 30 East; 717–393–3679), you can see thirty-two scenes that depict the history of Pennsylvania Dutch Country. See an animated barn-raising and such historical figures as Daniel Boone and Abraham Lincoln. Opens at 9:00 A.M. year-round seven days a week. Admission is $4.75 for adults, $3.00 for children five to eleven.

To see a typical Amish stone farm house, visit the **Amish Farm and House** (717–394–6185), only a half-mile east of Dutch Wonderland at 2395 Route 30 East. You can tour the farm with its barns, carriage sheds, spring-house, and animals. Open seven days a week at 8:30 A.M., the site closes at 4:00 P.M. in the winter, 5:00 P.M. in spring and fall, and 6:00 P.M. in the summer. Admission to Amish Farm and House is $5.00 for adults, $3.00 for children five to eleven.

Just outside of downtown Lancaster, there are two family oriented museums. "Greetings Earthlings!"—find out if you're fit and ready for a trip into space by visiting "Space Voyage Checkpoint," the newest exhibit at the **Hands-On House, Childrens' Museum of Lancaster** at 2380 Kissel Hill Road. The museum has eight other interactive areas for children ages two through ten. Admission is $4.00; the museum is open Tuesday, Wednesday, and Thursday from 11:00 A.M. to 4:00 P.M., Friday from 11:00 A.M. to 8:00

P.M., Saturday 10:00 A.M. to 5:00 P.M., and Sunday noon to 5:00 P.M. Admission to the Hands-On House is $9.00 for adults, $4.00 for children two to ten years of age. For information, call (717) 569–KIDS.

Cross the street from the Hands-On House to visit the **Landis Valley Museum.** This museum has an extensive collection of Pennsylvania Dutch items ranging from pottery to tools to guns. There are fifteen historic buildings including a farmhouse, a tavern, a country store, and a hotel. Open Tuesday through Saturday, 9:00 A.M. to 5:00 P.M., Sunday noon to 5:00 P.M. Closed Mondays and most holidays. Admission to the Landis Valley Museum is $7.00 for adults, $5.00 for children six to seventeen. Call (717) 569–0401 for information.

Downtown Lancaster is worth a visit, offering the Central Market, **"Newseum"** (the museum of Lancaster newspapers), **Steinman Park,** and more. A walking tour is available. For information, contact the Pennsylvania Dutch Convention and Visitors Bureau at (717) 299–8901 or (800) PA–DUTCH, ext. 4255.

The **Heritage Center of Lancaster County** is in downtown Lancaster at Penn Square. In the midst of all the quilts, furniture, folk art, and rifles, kids will be attracted to the **Hands-On Heritage Room,** where they can design their own quilt patterns or try out a sample archaeological dig. The museum and hands-on room are open at no charge year-round Tuesday through Saturday 10:00 A.M. to 4:00 P.M.

Next to the Heritage Center, breathe in the delicious smells of Amish baked goods coming from the **Central Market,** which has been operating as a farmers' market since the 1730s. It's open Tuesday through Friday 6:00 A.M. to 4:30 P.M. and Saturday from 6:00 A.M. to 2:00 P.M.

In spite of the pivotal role Pennsylvania played in our history, the Keystone State produced only one U.S. president, James Buchanan. Located on the outskirts of downtown Lancaster, **James Buchanan's Wheatland,** Buchanan's home, has been furnished with memorabilia of his life and career. The house, at 1120 Marietta Avenue in Lancaster, is open daily April through November 10:00 A.M. to 4:15 P.M. Call (717) 392–8721.

COLUMBIA

Water clocks, candle clocks, sundials, musical clocks, grandfather clocks, wristwatches, pocket watches. . . . You've never seen so many kinds of timepieces as you'll find at the **National Association of Watch and Clock Collectors Museum** at 514 Poplar Street just off Route 30 in Columbia (717–684–8261).

The sight of an Amish buggy may attract your children's curiosity, but it also presents a chance to learn to respect a very different way of living. (Courtesy Pennsylvania Dutch Convention and Visitors Bureau)

Parents of school-morning slugabeds will get inspiration from the alarm clock collection. For example, there's one alarm clock that gives the sleepyhead's big toe a yank. One tall musical clock runs seven days and plays seven different tunes. The museum is open Tuesday through Saturday 9:00 A.M. to 4:00 P.M. and Sunday from noon to 4:00 P.M. from May to September. Closed Mondays and holidays. Admission to the Watch and Clock Museum is $3.00 for adults, $1.00 for children six to seventeen.

Susanna Wright was known as the "bluestocking of the Susquehanna," but she was really more of a "Renaissance woman." (A "bluestocking" was a derogatory term for an intelligent unmarried woman.) Just a few blocks away from the Watch and Clock Museum at **Wright's Ferry Mansion** (Second and Cherry streets; 717–684–4325), you can get acquainted with this colorful but little-known character in American history. Wright operated a ferry here, drew up legal documents, raised silkworms, practiced medicine, and corresponded with people like Benjamin Franklin. Wright's home is open May through October, Tuesday, Wednesday, Friday, and Saturday from 10:00 A.M. to 3:00 P.M.

YORK

Our seven-year-old was disappointed to learn that kids under twelve are not allowed on the factory tours at Harley-Davidson, Inc.(1425 Eden Road; 717–848–1177). However, all ages are welcome at the adjacent **Harley-Davidson Museum,** where antique motorcycles on display include police bikes, army bikes, and bikes owned by celebrities. Museum tours are offered at specified times Monday through Friday. Plant tours are offered Monday through Friday 10:00 A.M. to 2:00 P.M. and are open to people over twelve. No cameras, no sandals allowed. Call ahead: (717) 848–1177.

HUMMELSTOWN

On your way to Hershey on Route 322, your young geologists can have a forty-five minute tour of **Indian Echo Caverns,** 368 Middletown Road (717–566–8131). You can also pan for gemstones at Gem Mill Junction, take a ride in a horse-drawn buggy, and pet the animals. Open daily except some holidays. Admission to the caverns is $7.00 for adults, $3.50 for children three to eleven.

HERSHEY

If ever there were a town made for family enjoyment, it's Hershey, Pennsylvania. What child could resist the city that chocolate built, with Hersheypark as its main attraction. Even the street lights are shaped like Hershey kisses! If you park your car at the Hersheypark Entrance, you can get around town on foot. Your first order of business will be a visit to **Hershey's Chocolate World Visitors Center** for a free ride on the chocolate-making tour. Even when the line here is long, it keeps moving. The ride gives an introduction to today's candy-making processes, and you'll get a free sample at the end.

The Chocolate World Visitors Center is open year-round at no charge from 9:00 A.M. to 4:45 P.M. In the summer it stays open until 6:45 P.M. Call (717) 534–4900 for details.

Next, of course, you'll want to do **Hersheypark,** which is located next to Chocolate World. As you enter, have your kids stand next to the "measure-up" signs. Kids of a certain height are "Hershey Kisses" and can ride "Hershey Kiss" rides. Taller kids are "Reeses Peanut Butter Cups," "Hershey Milk Chocolate Bars," "Twizzlers" or "Nutragious." If your kids would like to get a bracelet that shows what candy-height they are, you can stop by the rides office in the operations building, located inside the park beside "Swing Thing." (If you don't choose to get a bracelet, there are signs next to every

FAITH AND EMILY'S FAVORITE ATTRACTIONS IN HERSHEY–PENNSYLVANIA DUTCH COUNTRY

Hersheypark
Strasburg Railroad
National Railroad Museum
Museum of Scientific Discovery
State Museum of Pennsylvania
"Pride of the Susquehanna" Riverboat
"Cyclorama" at Gettysburg National Military Park
Fishing on the Yellow Breeches
Herr Food Factory

ride.) This manageable theme park is divided into small sections, which are centered around a different theme—and there's something for everyone. This way, your family can stay together and everyone can stay happy. For example, little ones can ride the "Swing Thing," which is a kid-sized version of "Wave Swinger." The antique carousel will delight many visitors while others flock to the "Comet" with its 95-foot drop. And don't stand anywhere near "Tidal Force" unless you don't mind getting wet! If you get hot and tired, a visit to the air-conditioned Music Box Theater may be just the ticket. If you do decide to split up, the "Kissing Tower" makes a good meeting spot.

Traveling with an infant, we were delighted to find that Hersheypark offers facilities for nursing mothers and baby food at the First Aid station. Even some of the men's rooms have changing tables.

Hersheypark's season runs from mid-May through mid-September. The gates open at 10:00 A.M. and the rides open at 10:30 A.M. Closing times vary from 6:00 P.M. to 11:00 P.M. Admission plans range from regular (ages nine to fifty-four) at $24.95 to junior and senior, both at $15.95. Children two and under are free, and the sunset savings plan (after 5:00 P.M.) is $13.95. Admission includes all rides, all live performances and a same-day visit to ZooAmerica, (see below). There is a separate charge for paddleboats and miniature golf. For further information, call (800) HERSHEY or (717) 534–3090.

Besides its regular season, Hersheypark opens for two special family events: Creatures of the Night at Halloween, and Hersheypark Christmas Candylane. At each of these events the park is specially lighted and decorated and most of the family-oriented rides are open.

You can enter **ZooAmerica North American Wildlife Park** (717–534–3860) directly through Hersheypark and admission to the zoo is included in your Hersheypark ticket. However, the zoo is open year-round, not just seasonally, and a separate admission is also available. ZooAmerica focuses on plants and animals from different regions in North America.

Many of Hershey's attractions grew out of Milton Hershey's special interests. The rose garden at the Hotel Hershey developed from his own passions for the flowers. ZooAmerica started out with the animals Hershey collected. And the Hershey Museum sprang from Hershey's original collection of artifacts.

The **Hershey Museum** (717–534–3439), administered by the Hershey Foundation, is located at the west end of Hersheypark Arena. Its permanent exhibits celebrate the history of Hershey—the town, its founder and its industries. Younger ones will enjoy the Discovery Room, which has hands-on activities on these themes. Admission to the museum is $4.25 for adults, $2.00 for youth, $3.75 for seniors.

You may want to check the schedule of events at **Hersheypark Stadium and Arena** (717–534–3911). Hershey also offers several golf courses, **Milton Hershey School,** and the **Derry One-Room School.**

Families will enjoy staying at either the Hotel Hershey or the Hershey Lodge. Both have indoor/outdoor pools, children's pools and free shuttle buses to Hersheypark. The lodge, however, has a playground and a less formal atmosphere.

The **Hotel Hershey** has two different restaurants to meet different tastes. Choose the Fountain Cafe if you're traveling with young children. While at the hotel, gardening enthusiasts should take time to smell the roses.

Outside of Hershey, there's yet another opportunity for your railroad buffs. Check out the scenic ride to Indian Echo caverns on the **Middletown and Hummelstown Railroad** (136 Brown Street, Middletown; 717–944–4435).

HARRISBURG

You can easily get around Pennsylvania's state capital on foot. It's convenient to park your car at the Walnut Street parking garage, located right at **Strawberry Square** (North Third and Market streets), an urban shopping mall with a food court and many shops.

Strawberry Square is also home to the **Museum of Scientific Discovery**

(717–233–7969), a hands-on science museum. The museum has clearly outgrown its limited space here, and there are major plans for expansion when it becomes part of the new Science and Arts Center across the street. The Museum of Scientific Discovery is open Tuesday through Friday 9:00 A.M. to 5:00 P.M., Saturday 10:00 A.M. to 5:00 P.M., and Sunday noon to 5:00 P.M. Closed Mondays. Admission is $5.00 for adults, $4.00 for children three to seventeen, $4.00 for seniors. Children under twelve must be accompanied by an adult.

Your young spelunkers can actually crawl on their hands and knees into a re-created limestone cave complete with stalagmites and stalactites and the sounds of dripping water. There is a brand-new planetarium, a preschool area, live animals, and "Virtual Arena," where for a small additional charge your kids can be heroes in a video game.

When you exit Strawberry Square, look up and you'll see the dome of the **State Capitol Building,** said to be the most impressive state capitol in the country. Inside, huge murals provide a "greatest hits" version of the history of Pennsylvania with scenes such as Penn's treaty with the Indians, the signing of the Declaration of Independence and Washington's troops at Valley Forge. The floors are made of tiles from the Moravian Pottery and Tileworks in Doylestown (see "Philadelphia Countryside"). The main floor of the rotunda displays over 350 flags once carried by regiments from Pennsylvania. The Capitol is open to the public daily from 9:00 A.M. to 4:00 P.M. You can pick up a brochure at the information desk.

The circular building to your right as you leave the Capitol is the **State Museum of Pennsylvania,** at Third and North streets (717–787–4978). This museum strives to describe the entire history and pre-history of the state. You'll work your way down, starting at the third floor. There you'll begin with geology and the earth and go on through paleontology, archaeology, and the beginning of civilization. In "Dino-Lab," you can observe a real paleontologist at work freeing a dinosaur skeleton from the rock. Using an intercom, you can ask questions about this painstaking process.

Going down to the second floor, you can see a series of life-sized dioramas depicting the life cycle of a Native American in this area. There are also displays about the Revolution and the Civil War, including a huge mural of the Battle of Gettysburg. One gallery re-creates a typical early American Main Street. In Curiosity Corner, younger children can try on antique clothing, handle birds nests, and use interactive computers.

On the first floor the museum displays its treasure, the original charter from the British crown that gave Pennsylvania to William Penn in 1681. This charter granted William Penn "rights, privileges and obligations" to Pennsylvania, as a payment of debts owed to Penn's father by King Charles

FAITH AND EMILY'S FAVORITE EVENTS IN HERSHEY– PENNSYLVANIA DUTCH COUNTRY

Kutztown Folk Festival, Schulykill County Fairgrounds, Summit
    Station (nine days surrounding July 4) (610) 683–8707
Pennsylvania Renaissance Faire (summer) (717) 665–7021
Charles Dickens Victorian Christmas (November through
    December) (717) 665–7021
Fort Hunter Day (September) (717) 599–5751
Hersheypark Christmas Candylane (November through
    December) (717) 534–3860 or (800) HERSHEY
Hersheypark "Creatures of the Night" (October) (717) 534–3860
    or (800) HERSHEY
Faerie Festival at the Rosemary House, Mechanicsburg
    (September) (717) 697–5111

II. It's amusing to note that Penn was to pay the king two beaver furs and all the gold and silver found in the colony. Of course, there was no gold or silver found in Pennsylvania.

The State Museum of Pennsylvania is open Tuesday through Saturday 9:00 A.M. to 5:00 P.M. and Sunday from noon to 5:00 P.M. It is closed holidays except for Memorial Day and Labor Day. Admission is free, but there is a small charge for Curiosity Corner and the planetarium show. By spring of 1996, a cafe will be open. The museum is handicapped-accessible.

If your feet aren't sore yet, you can walk over to the riverfront and cross **Walnut Street Bridge,** now exclusively for pedestrians. The bridge spans the Susquehanna River from Riverfront Park to City Island. (At night this bridge is illuminated, adding to the night-time view of the city.)

City Island sits in the middle of the Susquehanna, a spot of greenery amidst the water. Its sixty-three acres of park land now include **Riverside Stadium** where Class AA minor league baseball is played. You'll also find a steam-driven train for children, an arcade, miniature golf, jogging and skateboarding facilities, **HarbourTown,** and more.

From City Island, take a ride on the *"Pride of the Susquehanna"* (operated by Harrisburg Area Riverboat Society, 116 Pine Street; 717–234–6500). The riverboat tour gives an excellent view of this riverside city. Kids love looking up at the underside of the six bridges under which you'll pass, including the Walnut Street Bridge. Take your choice: You may sit indoors where there is a small snack bar, or on the lower or upper decks where the wind blows through your hair.

From the riverboat you can see the wrought-iron railing around the grave of the city's founder, John Harris. You can visit his home, the **John Harris/Simon Cameron Mansion,** at 219 South Front Street. This historic home was built in 1766 and now houses the collection of the Historical Society of Dauphin County.

Just outside Center City, on a bluff overlooking the Susquehanna River, stands **Fort Hunter Mansion** (5300 North Front Street; 717–599–5751), surrounded by its outbuildings and park. The Federal-style mansion was built in 1814 by Archibald McAllister and is in remarkably good condition. Touring the house, open the closet doors to discover surprises such as sets of china or collections of fashionable clothing left behind by Helen Reily, last owner of the house. In the guest room closet you can peek at Mrs. Reily's pantaloons, bonnets (she had some one hundred), fans, hat pins, and other accessories. She also left a collection of dolls, toy soldiers, and even paper dolls. The doll house features a tiny hobby horse, a little dog curled up in a minute dog bed, and postcards glued to the walls for paintings. And don't miss the garden with its spicebush, smokebush, and boxwoods.

Fort Hunter Mansion is open May through November, Tuesday through Saturday 10:00 A.M. to 4:30 P.M., Sunday noon to 4:30 P.M. In December, when the mansion is decorated for Christmas, it is open daily from noon to 7:00 P.M. In September, "Fort Hunter Day" brings the whole park alive with bagpipe music (in honor of the McAllisters), colonial art and crafts, food and more. Demonstrations of open-hearth baking are offered periodically, as are other special programs.

CARLISLE

At Carlisle, George Washington founded the Army's first arsenal and school, the **Carlisle Barracks.** Later this site served as the Indian School where Jim Thorpe received his education. Today the Carlisle Barracks houses the **U.S. Army War College.** History buffs won't want to miss the **Military History Institute** and **Omar N. Bradley Museum,** both in Upton Hall. The Military History Institute offers free tours of its collection of rare military books. Family historians can research family members who served in the armed forces. (It's helpful to know not only the name but the unit of your family member.) The Military History Institute and Bradley Museum are open weekdays only, 8:00 A.M. to 4:30 P.M. Closed weekends and federal holidays. For information call the Public Affairs office at (717) 245–4101.

Maybe somebody in your family is nuts about cars or antiques. The eighty-two-acre **Carlisle Fairgrounds** (1000 Bryn Mawr Road; 717–243–7855) hosts major collector events on many weekends throughout the year. The antiques shows take advantage of the abundance of antiques dealers based in this area, plus many from outside the county. The automobile shows offer car flea markets and car corral, as well as "new old stock," parts, and memorabilia. Special events include "Kids at Carlisle," in which children three to eight can show off their own miniature pedal-, battery-, or gas-powered cars. For a schedule of events, contact Carlisle Productions at (717) 243–7855.

For hiking, cross-country skiing, hunting, and other outdoor activities, contact **King's Gap Environmental Center** on Route 174 West (500 Kings Gap Road) at (717) 486–5031.

BOILING SPRINGS

The town of Boiling Springs has recently celebrated its sesquicentennial (150th birthday). This lovely lake-side town offers the **Allenberry Resort Inn and Playhouse** ("On the Yellow Breeches Creek," P.O. Box 7, Boiling Springs, 17007; 717–258–3211), an eighteenth-century estate where you can enjoy professional theater, fishing, and special events. The Allenberry stretch of the **Yellow Breeches** attracts many families to try their hand at fly-fishing. Here the rules are "catch and release" and "artificial lures only."

It's a little different on the **Letort Spring Run** (pronounced LEE-tort), which is considered more challenging and attracts many *A River Runs Through It* devotees. While in the area, enjoy the **Appalachian Trail,** or hike **King's Gap Environmental Center** or **Pine Furnace State Park.**

GETTYSBURG

Every schoolchild in America should get the chance to experience Gettysburg. Before your visit, older kids and parents can prepare by watching either Ken Burns's PBS "Civil War" series or the 1993 movie *Gettysburg.* You may also plan ahead by choosing a tour ahead of time. A tour will help you get a handle on this remarkable shrine. To find the one that best suits your needs and to receive a sixty-four-page booklet about Gettysburg, contact the Gettysburg Travel Council, Department R-67, Gettysburg 17325; (717) 334–

6274. You can also check with Battlefield Bus Tours, 778 Baltimore Street, Gettysburg 17325; (717) 334–6296.

The Gettysburg Travel Council recommends a minimum visit of three days to see all that Gettysburg has to offer. To prevent an overdose of history, plan for breaks and vary your activities. Here are some highlights:

Gettysburg National Military Park tells the story of those three days in July 1863. About 400 artillery guns stand along the Union and Confederate battle lines, and over 1,000 monuments help visitors picture what happened here.

Plan to stop at the **Visitor Center** first thing. Don't miss the Cyclorama, a 356-by-26-foot circular painting by Paul Phillippoteaux. You'll feel as if you're standing on the battlefield just before Pickett's charge. (Just think what an effect this painting must have had when it was completed in the 1880s!) Today a sound and light program brings the painting to life and adds to the experience. The Visitor Center also has an Electric Map of the battlefield and the **Museum of the Civil War,** the largest collection of Civil War artifacts anywhere.

Although admission to the park and Visitor Center are free, there is a small charge for the Cyclorama and Electric Map. Twenty-minute Cyclorama showings are offered every half hour from 9:00 A.M. to 4:30 P.M. The thirty-minute Electric Map showings are given every forty-five minutes from 8:15 A.M. to 4:15 P.M. For either show the fees are the same: Adults sixteen and over, $2.00; seniors, $1.50; children fifteen and under, free; group rate, $1.50.

There is a self-guided driving tour that takes about two or three hours. The park roads are open 6:00 A.M. to 10:00 P.M. Hikers, bikers, and horses are welcome. Licensed battlefield guides are also available from the National Park Visitor Center. Tours begin at 8:00 A.M. and depart hourly. The fee is $25.00 per car for each two-hour tour. Boy Scouts can earn a special merit badge by completing a 10-mile historic hike at Gettysburg.

Adjacent to the battlefield you'll find the **Eisenhower National Historic Site,** the 189-acre retirement home and farm of President and Mrs. Dwight Eisenhower. If you wish to tour the home, pick up tickets at the Gettysburg National Park Visitor Center, then take a shuttle bus to the Eisenhower farm. The farm is open daily from April through October. It is closed Monday and Tuesday from November through March, and for thirty-one days beginning the Sunday after New Year's Day. For information, call (717) 334–1124.

Pace yourself, because you've only just begun! You may wish to take a walking tour of downtown Gettysburg to get yourself oriented before visiting some of the many sites in town. The town's official **Information Center** is located at 35 Carlisle Street, across from Lincoln Square in the center of town.

Cross Lincoln Square from the Information Center to visit the **Lincoln Room Museum** (12 Lincoln Square; 717–334–8188). This is the room where Abraham Lincoln spent the night before he delivered the Gettysburg Address. The room is still furnished as it was that night. You can follow in Lincoln's footsteps with a ten-minute sound and light program and you can view original drafts of the famous speech. Open in the summer Monday through Thursday 9:00 A.M. to 7:00 P.M., Friday and Saturday 9:00 A.M. to 8:00 P.M. In the off-season, the museum is open Monday through Friday 10:00 A.M. to 3:00 P.M. Admission is $3.25 for adults, $1.75 for children.

After the Lincoln Room Museum, you may choose to turn left down Baltimore Street where most of the museums and sights are, or go right for a ride on the Gettysburg Steam Train.

Going down Baltimore Street away from Lincoln Square, you can stop at any of over ten points of interest, plus restaurants, shops, and galleries. Baltimore Street then forks. The left fork is the continuation of Baltimore Street, the right fork Steinwehr Avenue.

For something spookily different, hear stories by candlelight at **Farnsworth House Ghost Stories** at 401 Baltimore Street. In season, stories are given Tuesday through Friday at 9:30 P.M., and Saturday at 8:00 and 9:30 P.M. For details call (717) 334–8838. Hours vary seasonally. Call (717) 334–8838 for current schedule. Tickets are $5.00 for adults, children under six are free. Younger kids will enjoy a break from history at **Magic Town,** 49 Steinwehr Avenue. You'll want to look very closely at the minute details and "magic" illusions that make this tiny town seem so real. Open evenings. Call (800) 878–4276 or (717) 337–0492.

Continuing down Baltimore Street, you'll discover the **Jennie Wade House.** In addition to the thousands of men who died at Gettysburg, there was one woman. Twenty-year-old Jennie Wade was baking bread for the Union soldiers when she was hit by a stray bullet. You can see the bullet-hole at the Jennie Wade House at 758 Baltimore Street (717–334–4100). Admission is $5.25 for adults, $3.25 for children. A clever holographic display tells Jennie's story. Jennie Wade's house is adjacent to **Olde Town,** where the streets of Gettysburg of 1863 are re-created. The Jennie Wade House and Olde Town are open daily. In the summer, hours are 9:00 A.M. to 9:00 P.M., and in the off-season 9:00 A.M. to 5:00 P.M.

Baltimore Street is like a "museum row." At 529 Baltimore Street, the **Confederate States Armory and Museum** (across from the Holiday Inn and the Jennie Wade House) features many original Confederate weapons. For information call (717) 337–2340. The **Soldiers National Museum**

(777 Baltimore Street; 717–334–4890) has ten Civil War dioramas housed in the building that was General Howard's headquarters during the battle and later the Soldiers' National Orphanage.

You can hear U.S. presidents "speak" at the **Hall of Presidents and First Ladies,** also on Baltimore Street. A series of life-sized mannequins and taped messages can help kids learn the difference between Andrew Jackson and Andrew Johnson. The first ladies appear in reproductions of their inaugural gowns. Call (717) 334–5717 for information.

Going south on Steinwehr Avenue, you'll find more points of interest. At **The Conflict Theater,** 213 Steinwehr Avenue, **"Abraham Lincoln Speaks."** Award-winning actor Jim Getty portrays the president evenings at 8:00. In the summer performances are Monday through Friday. There are also performances during the July Fourth and Labor Day weekends, and on selected spring and fall dates. The Conflict Theater also offers six other Civil War programs, including **"Adventure at Gettysburg"** specifically designed for children. For information and reservations, call (717) 334–8003. Admission is $5.00 for adults, $4.00 for children.

The **National Civil War Wax Museum** at 297 Steinwehr Avenue has organized its more than 200 life-sized figures into an audiovisual presentation including thirty different scenes. You can see animated figures re-enact the Battle of Gettysburg and an animated Lincoln deliver the Gettysburg Address. On weekends from May until Labor Day, special events include living re-enactments. Admission fees: Adults, $4.50; young adults thirteen through seventeen, $2.50; children six through twelve, $1.75; children five and under, free. For information, call (717) 334–6245.

You can join Lincoln for the train ride to Gettysburg on a twelve-minute simulated trip at the **Lincoln Train Museum** on Steinwehr Avenue (717–334–5678). The museum also exhibits a toy train collection including a model railroad layout that represents the Civil War. Open in the summer from 9:00 A.M. to 9:00 P.M., and in the spring and fall 9:00 A.M. to 5:00 P.M. The museum is closed during the winter months. Admission to the Lincoln Train Museum is $5.25 for adults, $3.25 for children. The **Gettysburg Battle Theater,** 571 Steinwehr Avenue (717–334–6100), presents a film and multimedia re-enactment.

Board the **Gettysburg Railroad Train** at 106 North Washington Street (about 2 blocks from Lincoln Square) and choose between the 16-mile and 50-mile trips on trains that pass by the Gettysburg Battlefield. For schedules and fares, plus information about theme trains such as Civil War raids and the ride with Lincoln, call (717) 334–6932. Tickets cost $8.00 for adults, $4.00 for children.

Okay, so your younger ones have had enough history. Now's the perfect time to leave downtown Gettysburg and visit **Land of Little Horses,** 125 Glenwood Drive. The smallest Falabella horses may weigh seventy pounds and stand 20 inches high. Kids under eighty pounds can climb up on their backs (for an additional fee). The horses perform tricks four times a day, at 11:00 A.M., 1:00 P.M., 3:00 P.M., and 5:00 P.M. from Memorial Day through Labor Day. In spring and fall the 5:00 P.M. show is omitted. The Land of Little Horses is open April through October 10:00 A.M. to 5:00 P.M. In the summer hours are extended to 6:00 P.M. Call (717) 334–7259.

LAUREL HIGHLANDS REGION

The beauty of the Laurel Highlands area of Pennsylvania will take your breath away. One hundred miles of countryside, mountains, and valleys, two mountain ridges, and thirteen state parks and forests provide the setting for golfing, skiing, fishing, and hiking. The Youghiogheny River (the "Yock") means whitewater rafting, and Raystown Lake offers calmer boating, swimming, and more. In this area the Rails-to-Trails Conservancy is converting old railroad paths to hiking and biking trails. (For information, contact Rails-To-Trails of Central Pennsylvania at 814–832–2400 or Rails-To-Trails of Pennsylvania at 717–238–1717.)

Here you'll find a masterpiece of modern architecture, Frank Lloyd Wright's Fallingwater. Old Bedford Village re-creates our history, and Idlewild Park takes us to the Land of Make-Believe.

The Laurel Highlands is rich in history, especially sites associated with the French and Indian War, such as Fort Necessity and the authentically restored Fort Ligonier. In 1806, the National Road was built to link the East with what was then the Western frontier. This road is now Route 40, where every May wagoners with teams of horses commemorate the opening of the nation's first turnpike (the National Pike Festival). Two old tollhouses still exist along Route 40, which is also a great foliage route in October.

This area saw remarkable industrial development: coal mining, the steel industry, the growth of railroading, and the building of canals. Many families enjoy driving the 500-mile **Path of Progress Heritage Route,** which takes them past many of the sites described in this chapter. (For further information about the Path of Progress, call 800–898–3636.)

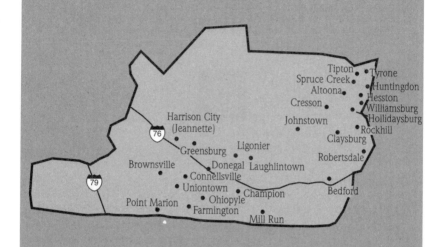

Tipton
Tyrone
Spruce Creek
Huntingdon
Altoona
Hesston
Cresson
Williamsburg
Hollidaysburg
Harrison City
(Jeannette)
Johnstown
Rockhill
Ligonier
Claysburg
Greensburg
Robertsdale
Donegal
Brownsville
Laughlintown
Connellsville
Uniontown
Champion
Bedford
Point Marion
Ohiopyle
Farmington
Mill Run

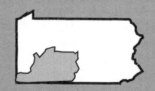

Laurel Highlands Region

POINT MARION

Friendship Hill National Historic Site is the home of Swiss-born patriot Albert Gallatin, who was elected to the U.S. Senate, played an important role in the Whiskey Rebellion, and later served in Congress, as Secretary of the Treasury, as a member of the team that negotiated the end of the War of 1812, and as minister to France.

The Brick House, the oldest portion of the home, was begun in 1789. Gallatin and subsequent owners of the house made improvements until about 1900. Friendship Hill is now being restored. You can tour the site at no charge any day 8:30 A.M. to 5:00 P.M. Guided tours take about twenty-five minutes, and there are also self-guided tours on compact disc.

There are 8 miles of trails and a picnic area. You can take a pleasant walk to the grave of Gallatin's first wife, Sophia Allegre. The site overlooks the Monongahela River, but watch out for the steep banks. Also, be aware that there may be potential dangers in old buildings and mine works that have not yet been restored. Since the house is sometimes closed for restoration work, it's wise to call ahead: (412) 725–9190.

Friendship Hill is in Point Marion, near New Geneva, off Route 119. It is open daily year-round 8:30 A.M. to 5:00 P.M. Closed Christmas Day.

FARMINGTON

At the **Fort Necessity National Battlefield** (412–329–5512), the young George Washington met with his first experience of battle, during the French and Indian War. Washington's forces won the first encounter. The fort was built afterward in expectation that the French would return, which they did, but this time Washington was forced into the only surrender of his career.

Today Fort Necessity has been reconstructed. At the Visitor Center here, you can view an audiovisual presentation about the fort, the battle, and the research behind the reconstruction effort. You'll probably be surprised when you see the size of the reconstructed fort. It is surrounded by a circular stockade 53 feet in diameter. The gate is only 3½ feet wide.

While you're in the neighborhood, you may wish to visit the **Mount Washington Tavern,** built in the 1820s on land once owned by the general himself. The tavern has been restored to look as it did originally, when it was constructed to serve travelers along the new National Road.

Fort Necessity Battlefield is 11 miles east of Uniontown, on Route 40 (the National Road). It is open every day from dawn to dusk. The Visitor Center and Mount Washington Tavern are open 8:30 A.M. to 5:00 P.M. Closed Christmas Day.

Located on a mountainside, **Laurel Caverns** (located 5 miles east of

Route 40, at the crest of Summit Mountain; 412–438–3003) offers not only the underground caves, but a breathtaking view.

Talk about family adventure! If you want, you can explore these caverns with only your map and flashlight to guide you. Watch your step in the narrow passageways. Bring your own flashlight, and don't forget spare batteries. Or you can take a guided tour.

At the end of the tour, don't miss the sound and light show, sort of an underground *Fantasia.* There's even an underground miniature golf course!

Open daily from May to October, 9:00 A.M. to 5:00 P.M. and weekends only in March, April, and November. Bring a jacket and a flashlight. Rappelling and climbing sessions are available to groups inside the caverns, as are fossil-hunting excursions.

UNIONTOWN

The U.S. government authorized construction of the National Road in 1806, to connect the East and the West. Even today it is the only road system constructed completely by the federal government. One of the National Road's toll-houses, **Searights Tollhouse,** is open to the public and is administered by Fayette County Historical Society. Inside the tollhouse, you can visit the toll keeper's office, kitchen, and living room. Open Tuesday through Saturday 10:00 A.M. to 4:00 P.M. and, from mid-May to mid-October, Sunday 2:00 to 6:00 P.M. Admission is $1.00 for adults, children are free. For information, call (412) 439–4422.

BROWNSVILLE

Despite its name, **Nemacolin Castle** (Front Street in Brownsville; 412–785–6882) is not a castle but the home of Jacob Bowman, who opened a trading post in Brownsville in 1786. It does look a little like a castle, though, with its turreted tower and battlements.

You can take a guided tour of twenty furnished rooms. Open Easter weekend 1:00 to 5:00 P.M., thereafter weekends 10:00 A.M. to 4:30 P.M. into October. In June, July, and August, it's also open Tuesday through Friday 11:00 A.M. to 4:30 P.M. Around the holidays, Christmas candlelight tours are offered.

CONNELLSVILLE

The Connellsville Area Historical Society (275 South Pittsburgh Street; 412–628–5640) administers **Crawford Cabin,** on North Seventh Street at the

---

FAITH AND EMILY'S FAVORITE ATTRACTIONS IN THE LAUREL HIGHLANDS AREA

Idlewild Park
Family Float Trip on Youghiogheny River
Laurel Caverns
Lincoln Caverns
Raystown Lake
Bat Hike in Canoe Creek Park
Rockhill Trolley Museum
Horseshoe Curve Railroad

Youghiogheny River. George Washington visited his lifelong friend Colonel William Crawford in this humble log cabin, 14 by 16 feet, built in 1765. Colonel Crawford and his men served Washington at the crossing of the Delaware and the battles of Trenton, Princeton, Brandywine, and Germantown. Call (412) 628–5640 for a recorded message describing hours and other information.

OHIOPYLE

Ohiopyle State Park's Youghiogheny River (affectionately nicknamed the Yough, pronounced "Yock") offers a wide range of river adventures. From March into October, thousands challenge the Yough. Find the guided or unguided trip that suits your family's taste and ages.

For novices or families with younger children, the Middle Yough is the best choice, with its gentler Class I and II rapids and relaxing scenery. Laurel Highlands River Tours offers a guided trip on the Middle Yough which they call their "Family Float Trip," for families with children four and up. (Many seniors also enjoy this trip.) Wilderness Voyageurs rents easily maneuverable rafts for unguided rafting. (See information on these establishments, below.)

The Lower Yough's Class III and IV rapids are a little wilder. The minimum age for this 7.5-mile stretch of the river is twelve years of age. Mountain Streams offers a mini-trip on the Lower Yough that lasts about two hours. Many of these organizations also provide bike rentals, kayaks, canoes, or "duckies." A duckie is sort of an inflatable kayak, used with a double-ended paddle, available with one or two seats. A Thrillseeker, also used with a double-ended paddle, is made of a harder plastic.

Teenagers with a taste for adventure can take on the Upper Yough. This 11-mile stretch of the river includes Class IV and V rapids, and is recommended for experienced paddlers only. The minimum age is sixteen.

Any of the following outfitters can help you select your trip: **Laurel Highlands River Tours,** P.O. Box 107, Ohiopyle 15470, (800) 4–RAFTIN/ (412) 329–8531; **Mountain Streams and Trails Outfitters,** P.O. Box 106, Route 381, Ohiopyle 15470, (800) RAFT NOW (723–8669); **White Water Adventurers, Inc.,** P.O. Box 31, Ohiopyle 15470, (800) WWA–RAFT; **Wilderness Voyageurs, Inc.,** P.O. Box 97 Department PA, Ohiopyle 15470, (800) 272–4141 or (412) 329–5517.

Ohiopyle is also the starting point for the **Laurel Highlands Hiking Trail.** You can hike 70 miles here from Ohiopyle to an area near Johnstown. Eight overnight sites have been set up along the trail, which is designed for serious hikers.

GREENSBURG

Archaeological research in Greensburg has revived **Hanna's Town.** A stockade fort, the home of Robert Hanna, the town jail, and a wagon shed are reconstructed. Klingensmith House has been moved here. You can visit the field museum and see archaeological artifacts unearthed here. Open Memorial Day through Labor Day, Tuesday through Sunday 1:00 to 5:00 P.M. In May, September, and October, it is open on weekends only.

Also in the area, you may want to check out the **Westmoreland Museum of Art** (221 North Main Street, 412–837–1500) or the **Westmoreland Symphony Orchestra** (412–837–1850).

HARRISON CITY (JEANNETTE)

Here's an opportunity to acquaint your family with a lesser-known conflict: Pontiac's War. In 1763 Native American forces under the command of war chief Pontiac struggled against the British, eventually occupying Fort Detroit and Fort Pitt. At the **Bushy Run Battlefield** (State Route 993 in Jeannette) the British turned the tide against this rebellion.

At the Visitor Center, an electric map helps you get your bearings. Take some time to observe the exhibits, maps, flags, and weapons and learn about this episode in our history. Then you can take a guided tour of the battlefield. There are 3 miles of historic hiking trails, education programs, and special events. On the Edge Hill Trail, each stop represents one aspect of the Battle of Bushy Run, including the Flour Bag Entrenchment in which flour bags were used to protect the British wounded.

Another trail, the Flour Sak Discovery Trail, focuses on how humans have used things from the forest. For example, the black walnut tree provided food, dye, insect repellent, gunstocks, and furniture.

The Iroquois Nature Trail was designed by the Boy Scouts to demonstrate the changes in the environment between the nineteenth and twentieth centuries. There are thirteen stations, such as "Beauty in Nature Through Adaptation," where you can see how nature has healed itself in what was once a stone quarry.

Open April through October. Museum: Wednesday to Saturday 9:00 A.M. to 5:00 P.M. and Sunday noon to 5:00 P.M. Battlefield: Wednesday to Sunday 9:00 A.M. to 5:00 P.M. From November to March the museum is closed and the battlefield is open Wednesday to Sunday 9:00 A.M. to 5:00 P.M. Admission is charged. Handicapped-accessible. Call (412) 527–5584.

DONEGAL

You can't drive past **Caddie Shak, Inc.** (412– 593–7400) without a reaction from your kids. ("Their tongues hang out," says one parent.) Convenient to the turnpike, Caddie Shak has Grand Prix go-carts, bumper cars, miniature golf, batting cages, games, and food. A nice way to break up the trip. Caddie Shak is located 1½ miles east on Route 31 off Exit 9 of the Pennsylvania Turnpike. Admission and parking are free. The rides and attractions are moderately priced and family discounts are available. Open March through October.

HIDDEN VALLEY

Hidden Valley Ski (4 Craighead Drive) wants you to learn to ski with them. One of the mid-Atlantic's most popular family ski resorts, Hidden Valley has seventeen ski slopes, 30 miles of cross-country ski trails, and a new half-pipe for snowboarders. They also have kids camp, indoor and outdoor pools, boating, fishing, tennis, and more. For details, call (814) 443–2600 or (800) 443–SKII.

CHAMPION

Snow Country and *Ski* magazines have rated **Seven Springs Mountain Resort** among the top fifty ski resorts in North America. This large facility offers lodging for over 5,000 people in hotel rooms, condos, and chalets. Besides ski and

snowboard rentals and ski lessons, they offer swimming, bowling, indoor miniature golf, and game rooms. Call (800) 452–2223 for information.

LAUGHLINTOWN

If you want to get a picture of what it was like in a typical roadside inn of the
eighteenth and nineteenth centuries, visit the **Compass Inn Museum,** 3
miles east of Ligonier, on Route 30 East in Laughlintown. The log part was built
in 1799 and the stone addition in 1820. The Ligonier Valley Historical Society
has restored the building, and the kitchen, blacksmith's shop, and barn have
been reconstructed on their original sites.

You can find out where terms like "upper crust" and "toasting" came
from. You can see how travelers spent the night crammed into beds with other
guests. You can visit the family's quarters, as well as the barn where old horse-
drawn and ox-drawn vehicles still remain, and sometimes a blacksmith is on
duty, demonstrating the craft. You can also see tools of the period.

The Compass Inn Museum is open May through October, Tuesday
through Saturday 11:00 A.M. to 4:00 P.M. and Sundays noon to 4:00 P.M.
During the summer, living history days are held on the third weekend of each
month. In November and December, candlelight tours are offered on weekends only. For information, call (412) 238–4983.

LIGONIER

Pronounce it "Lee-gon-EER."

"America's Most Beautiful Theme Park," **Idlewild Park** on Route 30
West (412–238–3666), is the home of Mister Rogers' Neighborhood of Make-
Believe, complete with the Neighborhood Trolley your preschoolers have
always wanted to see. Fred Rogers himself served as creative consultant for this
charming replica with the castle, King Friday, Queen Sarah Saturday, and all the
details you'll recognize right away.

This relaxing and manageable park, nestled in the woods, is perfect for
children twelve and under. But it also has rides for older kids. Located about 50
miles east of Pittsburgh and also a sister park to Kennywood and Sandcastle, it
began as a picnic area in 1878. Today the three-row carousel, built by
Philadelphia Toboggan Company in the 1930s still entrances children of all ages.

You'll literally step through the pages of a Story Book to visit the homes
of "Peter, Peter, pumpkin eater," "The Three Little Pigs," and the "Little
Crooked Man," among others. The beloved Story Book Forest was added in
1956, with its over forty scenes and characters from fairy tales and nursery
rhymes. In fact, since the Story Book Forest was built, only two women have

"He bought a crooked cat, which caught a crooked mouse,/And they all lived together in a little crooked house.." This nursery rhyme comes to life at Idlewild Park's Story Book Forest. (Courtesy Idelwild Park)

portrayed the Woman Who Lived in a Shoe. The current Woman has played the role for a number of years, as her mother did before her. It takes about an hour to explore the Story Book Forest.

A relatively new attraction, Jumpin' Jungle gets families climbing and crawling and, well, jumping. Climb up the netting, jump in the ball room. H_2Ohhh Zone is a giant water attraction for all ages. It has body flumes, "shotgun" slides, and a huge swimming pool, plus Little Squirts, wet fun for younger ones.

Admission to Idlewild Park, which includes all rides and attractions is a real bargain: $13.95 for anyone aged two to fifty-four; $7.00 for seniors; children two and under are free.

The park is open Tuesday through Sunday, June through August, on weekends only mid-May to June and on holiday Mondays. The gates open at 10:00 A.M. and closing times vary. Bring your bathing suit if you plan to go on any of the water slides or swim in the pool.

Fort Ligonier was built by the British during the French and Indian War. The entire fort, except for its foundation, was destroyed by 1800, but has been carefully reconstructed. It has gun batteries and a retrenchment. The Visitor Center offers exhibits and a film. You can visit several restored buildings such as a quartermaster's storehouse, magazine, hospital, and commissary.

Every October, on the anniversary of its most famous battle, the fort celebrates Fort Ligonier Days. The fort is open daily April to October, 9:00 A.M. to 5:00 P.M. Call (412) 238–9701 for further information.

This beautiful area is really something to see from the air. **Windswept "Hot Air Balloon" Adventures,** 303 Chrisner Road, offers both morning and evening flights. Children eight to twelve must be accompanied by an adult, and children weighing under sixty pounds fly at half-price. If one member of your family doesn't want to fly, he or she can follow the balloon with the chase crew, which is also fun. For further information and pricing schedule, call (412) 238–2555. Make your reservations early.

MILL RUN

The story goes that Frank Lloyd Wright told Edgar Kaufmann, "I want you to live with the waterfall, not just look at it." Because of the technology of cantilevers, Wright was able to do just that.

In a beautiful wooded setting, Wright placed **Fallingwater,** one of his most significant architectural achievements. It seems as if it has always been here, with the waterfall cascading from it. Inside the house, walls of windows look out into the woods. The American Institute of Architects has called Fallingwater "the best all-time work of American architecture."

The regular tour takes about forty-five minutes, but if you like you may make a reservation for a longer tour, which is very detailed and can take up to two hours.

Please note that children under nine are not permitted to take the regular tour of the house. However, if you wish to see it yourself, you may take advantage of child care provided here ($2.00 per child per hour). If you have children six to nine who might like to see the house, call to find out when special children's tours are scheduled. Reservations are recommended for both children's and adult tours. Call (412) 329–8501 for reservations and information.

Fallingwater is open for guided tours April to mid-November, Tuesday through Sunday 10:00 A.M. to 4:00 P.M. In the winter, tours are offered weekends only 11:00 A.M. to 3:00 P.M. Tours are $8.00 per person, and do require a fair amount of walking. Only the first floor is handicapped-accessible. Lunch is available in Fallingwater's restaurant.

Fallingwater is operated by the Western Pennsylvania Conservancy, which also runs **Bear Run Nature Preserve,** one-half mile away. It is very convenient to Ohiopyle.

The family can camp at **Yogi Bear's Jellystone Park,** but even if you're not camping here, you can take advantage of the water slides, playground, and other recreational activities. For information and pricing schedule, call (800) HEY–YOGI.

JOHNSTOWN

The town of Johnstown will always be remembered as the site of the tragic flood that occurred on May 31, 1889. The stress of a storm proved too much for the town's neglected dam, which broke, sending a wall of water down the mountain and through the town, killing more than 2,000 people.

The Johnstown Flood began on the site in Saint Michael where you can see the **Johnstown Flood National Memorial,** administered by the National Parks Service. In fact, you can see what little is left of the South Fork Dam from here. A weakness in this dam is suspected of making the flood so disastrous.

An award-winning documentary, *Black Friday,* brings the events to life. The thirty-five-minute film puts you inside the terror of the flood. In fact, it is so effective parents are warned that it may be too frightening for young children.

The Memorial is open at no charge from Memorial Day to Labor Day, 9:00 A.M. to 6:00 P.M. During the rest of the year, it is open 9:00 A.M. to 5:00 P.M. It is closed on major holidays. In the summer you can see re-enactments of some of the events surrounding the flood. You can also take a tour around the dam. The flood happened on Memorial Day, so every year during that holiday weekend, the abutments of the dam glow with the light of thousands of luminaries. Special presentations are offered, including "Tales of the Great Flood." Call (814) 495–4643 for details.

After visiting the Memorial, you'll want to complete the story with a tour of the Johnstown Flood Museum. But first you might want to break up the seriousness with an exhilarating ride on the **Johnstown Inclined Plane,** at 711 Edgehill Drive. You'll travel up on an amazing 71.9 percent grade, the steepest vehicular inclined plane in the world. Your car can ride the incline with you, if you desire, so that you can drive around the town of Westmont.

After the Johnstown Flood, the frightened residents of the area wanted to live at the top of the hill, but they needed a way to commute to and from the city, so this incline was built. An "incline" is an unusual kind of cable railway found in Johnstown and Pittsburgh. During Johnstown's two subsequent floods (1962 and 1977), the incline became the people's escape route. At night, when both the tracks and the cars are lit up, the incline is a spectacular sight.

At the top of the incline, there is an observation deck, Visitor Center, and the Incline Station Restaurant and Pub. From this vantage point, you can see one of the largest American flags anywhere.

On weekdays the ride runs from 6:30 A.M. to 10:00 P.M. On Saturday, its hours are 7:30 A.M. to 10:00 P.M., and on Sunday, 9:00 A.M. to 10:00 P.M. Call (814) 536–1816 for fares and schedules. Free parking is available at both the top and the bottom.

The **Johnstown Flood Museum,** 304 Washington Street, tells the story of the disaster. Photos show how the town looked before the waters came, and after. An animated map with light and sound effects shows how the water swept through Johnstown, destroying thousands of homes and businesses.

First, see the documentary film *The Johnstown Flood,* which won the Academy Award for Best Documentary Short Subject in 1989. This twenty-five-minute movie was made using black-and-white still photos taken after the flood. A longer version of this movie has been shown on PBS's "The American Experience."

Then visit the two floors of permanent exhibits. The third floor is used for temporary exhibits, such as one describing Johnstown's many ethnic "clubs."

The museum is located in the 107-year-old Carnegie Library. It is open May though October, Sunday to Thursday 10:00 A.M. to 5:00 P.M.; Friday and Saturday 10:00 A.M. to 7:00 P.M. From November to April it is open 10:00 A.M.

At the Johnstown Flood Museum, you can watch an animated map display that shows the path of the flood that swept through the city on May 31, 1889. (Courtesy Johnstown Area Heritage Association)

to 5:00 P.M. Call (814) 539–1889 for information and admission charges.

Tracks Through Time, a narrated train ride from Johnstown to Altoona, follows the path of the Johnstown flood wave. From early June until mid-October, Park Service rangers take you around the Horseshoe Curve, telling the story of the flood. Although you can ride either way between the two cities, round-trips are available only from Johnstown to Altoona and then back to Johnstown. During the layover in Altoona, you can visit the Railroaders Memorial Museum and other sites in the area. For schedules and information, call (814) 946–1100 in Altoona or (814) 535–3313 in Johnstown.

Every September, the Johnstown Area Heritage Association hosts **Johnstown FolkFest,** three days of music and culture reflecting the historical and ethnic heritage of the area. For information, call (814) 539–1889.

CLAYSBURG

Blue Knob Recreation (PA Turnpike Exit 11 to Route 20 North), one of the top ski resorts in the area, offers a KinderSki program, ski school, outdoor ice rink, swimming pools, and both junior and senior rates. For details, call in-state (800) 822–3405 or (814) 239–5111. Out-of-state, call (800) 458–3403.

CRESSON

In the middle of the nineteenth century, when Philadelphia was being linked to Pittsburgh by rail and canal, this portion of the Allegheny Mountains between Hollidaysburg and Johnstown seemed impassable. So someone came up with a "portage railroad" (not Rube Goldberg, although it almost looks as if it could be his work). A series of inclines carried the freight and passengers up the hills.

At the **Allegheny Portage Railroad National Historic Site** you can see a film, model, and exhibits that explain how this system worked. The railroad no longer exists, but you can walk along a portion of its route and see one section of restored track. As you enjoy the view from the overlook, be sure to note Skew Arch Bridge, which is actually twisted so that a wagon road could pass over the track.

The Allegheny Portage Railroad Site is located 12 miles west of Altoona and 10 miles east of Ebensburg on Route 22, off the Gallatzin exit. It is open Memorial Day through Labor Day 9:00 A.M. to 6:00 P.M. The rest of the year it is open 9:00 A.M. to 5:00 P.M. Closed Christmas Day. Call (814) 886–6150. Admission is free.

TIPTON

Bland's Park (Old Route 220) has something for everyone, even if your family includes a toddler. Rides, miniature golf, pony rides, bumper cars, and much more are available for family fun. Open daily except Mondays from early June through Labor Day, weekends in May and September. For information, call (814) 684–3538. Admission is free!

ALTOONA

Altoona has a lot to offer. Once known as a great railroad town, Altoona had several large railroad shops. Several of the shop buildings still remain. There are many museums devoted to the technology of railroading, but the **Altoona Railroaders Memorial Museum** (1300 Ninth Avenue) tells the story of the *people* involved in this gigantic industry. You'll see the rolling stock still waiting in the yard outside the Master Mechanics Building where the museum is housed, once part of the Pennsylvania Railroad. Inside, a locomotive dominates the lobby. As you enter you'll receive an ID card. Admission to the museum is $3.50 for adults, $3.00 for seniors, $2.00 for children three to twelve. Children under three are free and groups of four or more are eligible for a ten percent discount.

Your first order of business is the theater presentation about the people of the Pennsylvania Railroad. Next, you'll really get a feel for what it was like to live in a railroad town. You can visit a typical railroader's home, or see how safety was maintained by testing in the Altoona railroad lab. You can hear the voices of the workers and their families. Many exhibits are hands-on.

The museum is open daily May through October, 10:00 A.M. to 6:00 P.M. From November to April, the museum is open 10:00 A.M. to 5:00 P.M. Call (814) 946–0834 for further information.

At the Altoona Railroaders Museum, you can see a film that describes how the Horseshoe Curve Railroad was built. Then you can drive about 5 miles to watch the trains at **Horseshoe Curve National Historic Landmark.** Also administered by the Altoona Railroaders Museum, this incredible engineering feat made the Allegheny Portage Railroad obsolete (see above).

You can watch the trains go by from the Visitor Center, where you can also see a model of what the area looked like before the railroad changed the landscape. The best view of the trains is from above. You can get there by funicular or on foot.

Open at no charge daily May through October 9:30 A.M. to 7:00 P.M. and November through April 10:00 A.M. to 4:30 P.M. Closed on Mondays. Funicular rides are $1.50 round-trip. Call (814) 946–0834.

Many people don't know that Conrail and Amtrak still have trains on this track, which is unchanged since it was opened in 1854. You can ride the train around Horseshoe Curve, but you can't board it at the Visitor Center. Trains run between Johnstown and Altoona.

During the summer season, the National Park Service offers **Tracks Through Time,** a narrated train ride from Johnstown to Altoona, passing through Horseshoe Curve. Although you can ride either way between the two cities, round-trips are available only from Johnstown to Altoona to Johnstown. For schedules and information, call (814) 946–1100 in Altoona or (814) 535–3313 in Johnstown.

Kids love exploring closets and attics, and they're welcome to snoop around in the **Quaint Corner Children's Museum** (2000 Union Avenue, only a few blocks from the Railroad Museum). Peek in the International Closet or the Amish Closet, and climb up the ladder to Grandma's Attic.

The Quaint Corner Children's Museum was designed as a place for families to explore together, promoting creative hands-on learning and an appreciation for art, history, and science. The Audubon Room is chock-full of animals, starting with the bear rugs on the floor. The Period Room re-creates the world of a nineteenth-century child. One unusual feature is "Can You See What I See?" in which children can put on special glasses that help them experience the world of the visually-impaired. Puppets, dress-up clothes, doll houses, and a new doll collection round out this museum. There's even a player piano in the gift shop.

The museum is a bargain at $1.00 for children, $1.50 for adults. It is open Saturdays from 1:00 to 5:00 P.M. Call (814) 944–6830.

Ironmaster Elias Baker built his Greek revival–style mansion with local limestone and iron from his own furnace. The **Baker Mansion Museum** reflects the family's luxurious life style. Kids get a kick out of contraptions like the dumbwaiter and the speaking tubes used to talk to the servants. An important governors' conference took place here during the Civil War, so today the Lincoln Room displays Civil War artifacts and information about this conference. You can also see a servant's bedroom and a nursery full of antique toys. Open weekends in mid-April, May, September, and October 1:00 to 4:30 P.M. From June through Labor Day, the museum is open daily except Mondays and holidays. Hour-long tours depart regularly until 3:30 P.M. Call (814) 942–3916 for information.

Operated by a third generation of the Benzel family, **Benzel's Pretzel Bakery** (5200 Sixth Avenue, Route 764) makes about five million pretzels every day. Once the pretzels were shaped by hand, but today the dough goes through an extruder. The factory is open to the public Monday through Thursday 9:00 A.M. to 5:00 P.M., Friday 9:00 A.M. to 6:00 P.M., and Saturday

9:00 A.M. to 1:00 P.M. Tours are free. Call (814) 942–5062 for information. To order pretzels by mail, call (800) 344–GIFT.

Altoona is also the home of **James Industries, Inc.**—the makers of Slinky! In the past, tours of the factory were offered but this is no longer available. There is an outlet store, however.

Cast your cares away at **Lakemont Park,** 700 Park Avenue. Waterslides, bumper cars, go-carts, miniature golf, rides of all types including "Spins n' Grins" Kiddieland. Lakemont Park is open daily from June to August, and open weekends in May and September, 11:00 A.M. to 9:00 P.M. For details, call (814) 949–PARK.

WILLIAMSBURG

To find out about railroad tracks that have been converted to hiking and biking trails, contact **Rails-to-Trails of Central Pennsylvania** at (814) 832–2400. Williamsburg is a town that prizes its historical and architectural heritage. Groups can arrange in advance for a variety of tours offered by the **Williamsburg Heritage and Historical Society,** Williamsburg High School, West Third Street, Williamsburg 16693; (814) 832–2125.

SINKING VALLEY

In Sinking Valley, between Altoona and Tyrone, you can visit the site of another fort, **Fort Roberdeau.** This 1778 stockade has been reconstructed and now offers living history re-enactments, tours, and a picnic area. Open May 15 through September 30, Tuesday to Saturday 11:00 A.M. to 5:00 P.M. and Sunday 1:00 to 5:00 P.M. Closed on Mondays. For information, call (814) 946–0048.

TYRONE

A sweet taste of nostalgia for children of all ages, **Gardners Candies,** 30 West Tenth Street, has been making candies for nearly a century. Inside its History of Candyland Museum, you can visit a penny candy store complete with big jars of colorful penny candies such as fireballs, licorice, and candy buttons. It looks right out of a picture book, with dark wood candy counter, Tiffany-style lamp, brass scales, and antique valentine hearts.

You can see a movie about the family-owned business and how candy-making has changed over the years. In the candy kitchen you can see the old-fashioned tools of the trade—copper kettles, a marble counter, taffy hooks, peanut roasters, and chocolate molds. And of course you can select from more than 300 varieties of Gardners' candies, chocolates, home-style cooked nuts, and hand-dipped ice cream.

Gardners Candies is open Monday through Saturday 9:30 A.M. to 9:00 P.M. and Sunday from 1:00 to 9:00 P.M. Admission is free. Call (814) 684–0857.

SPRUCE CREEK

There are real cave paintings on the walls of **Indian Caverns** in Spruce Creek: a turtle, a tepee, a Mohawk chief.

More than 400 years ago, Native Americans used these caverns as a winter shelter, council chamber, and burial ground. Adjacent to Indian Caverns is a second cavern, **Giant's Hall**, where you can view the Grotto of the Wah Wah Taysee, a cave that glows, and the Frozen Niagara, more than two stories tall. Kids enjoy the sounds made by a musical rock.

The wide concrete walkways and Native American artifacts make this an excellent cavern if your family includes a wide range of ages, attention spans, and energy levels.

Indian Caverns is located 11 miles east of Tyrone on Route 45, between Waterstreet and State College in Huntington County. During the summer, hours are 9:00 A.M. to 6:00 P.M. daily. In April, May, September, and October, hours are 9:00 A.M. to 4:00 P.M. daily. November through March, the cavern is open weekends only, 9:00 A.M. to 4:00 P.M. Call (814) 632–7578 for information.

HOLLIDAYSBURG

If you want to stay in comfort in a beautiful forested setting, Trough Creek Cottage, at **Trough Creek State Park,** is available for rental year-round. It is a two-story home built in the 1800s as an ironmaster's house, and now completely renovated, including a modern eat-in kitchen, four bedrooms, bathroom, and central heat. For information and pricing schedule, call (814) 658–3847.

You can reserve either a rustic or modern cabin and enjoy a wide variety of nature education programs at **Canoe Creek State Park**, located on Route 22, about 13 miles east of Altoona, and about 7 miles east of Hollidaysburg or 11 miles west of Water Street; (814) 695–6807.

Canoe Creek State Park is one of a few parks that offer bat hikes, a favorite with our boys. At Canoe Creek, you can join in on a bat hike to look in on Pennsylvania's largest bat nursery colony (females and young) in the attic of an old church. As night falls they emerge from their home—about 10,000 of them! Children under twelve must be accompanied by an adult. Bring a flashlight. Other programs teach about bluebirds, birds' nests, frogs and toads, and wildflowers. Persons with a disability may call (814) 695–6807 if assistance will be needed to participate in the program.

Hollidaysburg also happens to be the home of the **Path of Progress Route.** For information, call (800) 898–3636.

FAITH AND EMILY'S FAVORITE EVENTS IN THE LAUREL HIGHLANDS AREA

Overly Country Christmas (November through December) (412) 423-1400

Hidden Valley Resort Winter Carnival (late January) (814) 443-2600 or (800) 443-SKII

Seven Springs Resort Spring Festival (March) (800) 452-2223

Ligonier Scottish Highland Games, Idlewild Park (September) (412) 238-3666

National Pike Festival (October) (412) 329-1560

Fort Ligonier Days (October) (412) 238-4200

Pioneer Days, Old Bedford Village (September) (814) 623—1156

HUNTINGDON

Greenwood Furnace State Park, less than forty minutes from Huntington, Lewistown, or State College, is a green park area on the site of the Greenwood iron furnaces and the "village built around an inferno." You can take a one-hour self-guided walking tour of a portion of the historic district, and see parts of the town such as the tramway, historic roads, and charcoal hearths. The Visitor Center is open daily from Memorial Day weekend through Labor Day, 9:00 A.M. to 5:00 P.M. During spring and fall, the center is open limited hours. Campsites are available. Call (814) 667-3808.

Lincoln Caverns and Whisper Rocks on Route 22, 3 miles west of Huntington, are a bit more challenging than some other nearby caverns. The walkways are narrow, wet, and steep, but the rock formations are spectacular: flowstones, stalactites, calcite, and crystals.

Ann Dunlavy Molosky, third-generation manager of the cave, emphasizes education as well as fun. Many educational programs are available, including geology and speleology workshops, as well as programs focused on debunking common misconceptions about bats.

A single admission fee gets you into Lincoln Caverns and Whisper Rocks. The cave is open daily Memorial Day through Labor Day 9:00 A.M. to 7:00 P.M. In April, May, September, October, and November, hours are open 9:00 A.M. to 5:00 P.M. Bring a sweater. Call (814) 643-0268.

The **Swigart Museum** (Route 22 East; 814–643–0885) owns the impressive collection of W. Emmert Swigart, one of the earliest collectors of old automobiles. (The museum's current director is one of his descendants.) Swigart was especially interested in cars manufactured by smaller companies, such as a 1906 Firestone Columbus, a 1907 Jewel, and the only remaining Carroll.

About forty cars from the museum's collection of 200 are generally on view. The museum also has the world's largest collection of name plates and license plates. Kids will be interested in the exhibit of antique toy cars, trains, and dolls.

Located on Route 22, 4 miles east of Huntington, the museum is open daily in June, July, and August, 9:00 A.M. to 5:00 P.M., and weekends only in May, September, and October, 9:00 A.M. to 5:00 P.M.

ROCKHILL FURNACE

East Broad Top Railroad (Route 994, 1 mile west of Orbisonia in Rockhill Furnace; 814–447–3011) once carried coal and other raw materials. Today it is the most complete and authentic rail site in North America.

Take a guided walking tour of the rail yard and roundhouse, then board the train for a ride on the only narrow-gauge railroad in the East still running at its original site. The narrated train ride takes about fifty minutes and carries you past countryside that is virtually unchanged since the days when East Broad Top Railroad transported coal along these tracks. If you like, bring along a picnic lunch. You can get off at Colgate Grove, picnic, and go back on a later train.

Open from Memorial Day weekend to mid-October, Tuesdays through Sundays with three train trips daily and two guided walking tours.

Adjacent to East Broad Top Railroad, you can visit the **Rockhill Trolley Museum** on Meadow Street (Route 994). This museum has twenty-six trolleys and streetcars, including cars from Norristown, Philadelphia, Johnstown, Harrisburg, Scranton, and York. You can take a 2½ mile ride on a restored trolley, passing the **Rockhill Iron Furnace.**

Like the National Trolley Museum near Pittsburgh, the Rockhill Museum is staffed by volunteers who love what they're doing. Volunteers here are members of Railways to Yesterday, Inc. Your trolley ticket is good for unlimited rides on the date purchased. Most days, you can try out two or three different cars. You can bounce along on the Toonerville Trolley or enjoy the fresh air in "1875" which is open on the sides.

Fares are $3.00 for adults, $1.00 for children. Open daily from Memorial

Day to mid-October, 10:30 A.M. to 4:30 P.M., plus some weekends and holidays. Trolleys operate 11:00 A.M. to 4:30 P.M. On weekends, the number to dial is (814) 447–9576; other days call (717) 263–3943 or (610) 965–9028 for information. Or you can write to Railways to Yesterday, Inc., P.O. Box 1601, Allentown 18105.

HESSTON

Area residents believe that **Raystown Lake** doesn't get the attention it deserves. This huge man-made lake is located in Huntington County, surrounded by two state forests, trout-stocked streams, museums, historic sites, campgrounds, and lots of family recreation. Call (814) 658–3405 or (800) RAYSTOWN.

There are several ways to see the lake and its countryside. **Seven Points Cruises** offers a number of different cruises, including special **Kidz Kruz** on its two excursion boats, the *Raystown Belle* and the *Raystown Queen.* You get a view of the lake including Sheep Rock Cliffs, a box lunch, a chance to feed the fish, and a demonstration of the "rack storage" building in which over 200 hundred boats are kept.

The boats operate for both private charter and for the public, April through October. Public cruises depart up to three times a day at the height of the season, and cost $6.00 for adults, $5.00 for seniors, and $2.50 for children under twelve. Call (814) 658–3074 for departure times and details.

You can also take a paddlewheel boat ride on the ***Proud Mary,*** which sails on Raystown Lake. This is also a great spot for recreation like swimming, fishing, hiking, and more. Lake Raystown Resort and Lodge, where the *Proud Mary* docks, also has a water park, an inner tube ride, and children's activity pool. For information, call (814) 658–3500, (800) RAYSTOWN, or (800) 628–4262.

ROBERTSDALE

In the Reality Theater on Main Street in Robertsdale, the **Broad Top Area Coal Miners Museum and Entertainment Center** offers exhibits about coal mining and railroading in the area. Open Saturdays 10:00 A.M. to 5:00 P.M. and Sundays 1:00 to 5:00 P.M. Call (814) 635–3807, 635–3220, or –2013.

BEDFORD

If you like the tradition of stealing a kiss on a kissing bridge, you'll love Bedford County. It has fourteen covered bridges and you can cuddle your toddlers and embarrass your older kids on every one of them.

Drive over the Amish Kissing Bridge to **Old Bedford Village,** Business Route 220, one-half mile south of PA Turnpike Exit 11. The village is also reachable via Route 30, the scenic Lincoln Highway.

This restored village of more than forty log structures is beautifully laid out to re-create a typical village with homes, schools, a church, and shops. Interpreters in authentic costumes bake bread and make brooms, baskets, and pottery. The kids will love stopping for ice cream or donuts as you tour the town. Call (814) 623–3335 if you wish to see a play in the village's **Log Opera House.** Meals are available at **Pendergrass Tavern** in the village.

Open daily starting on the second Sunday in April until the last Sunday in October, 9:00 A.M. to 5:00 P.M. Call (814) 623–1156 for information. Admission is $6.95 for adults, $5.95 for seniors, $4.95 for children six and over. Annual special events include a crafts festival in June, gospel music in August, Civil War re-enactments in September, pumpkin festivals in October, and a holiday celebration in December. In 1995, for the first time the Village offered a storytelling festival in August.

You can take a pleasant walking tour of Historic Downtown Bedford, including several historic houses and the Fort Bedford Museum. Fort Bedford is gone, but you can learn about its past by touring the **Fort Bedford Museum** (Fort Bedford Drive, 814–623–8891). The museum includes a scale model of the fort, Native American artifacts, weapons, uniforms, a Conestoga wagon, and children's toys of the period. The museum is open May through October 10:00 A.M. to 5:00 P.M. In May, September, and October it is closed on Tuesdays.

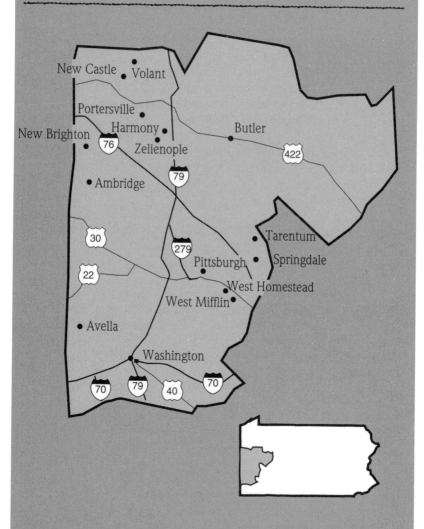

Pittsburgh and
Environs

PITTSBURGH AND ENVIRONS

From the dizzying height of one of its two inclines with the city spread below you, to the *Gateway Clipper* riverboat from which you see the city at the confluence of the Monongahela, Allegheny, and Ohio rivers, Pittsburgh comes as a pleasant surprise. As the boat passes the tip of Point State Park, you'll see a striking fountain that shoots a blast of water straight up into the sky.

Entering Pittsburgh through the Fort Pitt Tunnel, you'll see why the *New York Times* has called this "the only city in America with an entrance." Pittsburgh has the "Golden Triangle" (downtown area) with the cleanest free subway system in the United States, and the brand-new "Wayfinder" system of 1,500 brightly colored signs to help you navigate.

For one hundred years, the names Pittsburgh and Carnegie have been inextricably linked. Andrew Carnegie believed that wealth should be used to benefit the public. Thanks to Andrew Carnegie, and the museums he helped to create, your trip to Pittsburgh can include dinosaur bones, paintings, sculpture, a submarine, and more. Celebrating its centennial in 1996, the Carnegie museums include the Carnegie Science Center, Museum of Art, Museum of Natural History, Library of Pittsburgh, Music Hall and Performing Arts Center, and the Andy Warhol Museum.

You'll also benefit from the legacies of some of Pittsburgh's other leading families: the Mellons, Fricks, and Phippses.

And then, within minutes, you can be squealing with excitement at America's favorite traditional amusement park or at an outstanding waterpark.

DOWNTOWN PITTSBURGH

Start your adventure in downtown Pittsburgh with a stop at the Visitor Center on Liberty Avenue near Stanwix Street, a handy place to pick up maps, brochures, and advice. Just a few blocks away, near the intersection of Wood Street and Boulevard of the Allies, at 10 Children's Way, is the **Pittsburgh Children's Museum (PCM).**

The beloved characters of *Mister Rogers' Neighborhood*—King Friday the Thirteenth, Queen Sarah Saturday, and, of course, the Neighborhood Trolley—originate in Pittsburgh on WQED-TV. Kids can see them "in person" at the PCM. This hands-on museum is aimed at children twelve and under, and is located in the historic Old Post Office building. Kids can learn about language arts, mind and motor skills, local history, cultural diversity, and good health. Youngsters will also enjoy seeing Jim Henson's characters from films such as *The Dark Crystal* and *Labyrinth,* as well as PCM's own 7-foot-tall mascot "Stuffee."

An original print by Andy Warhol serves as inspiration as your kids cut a stencil to make their own silkscreen to take home. Then they can climb up and slide down on "Luckey's Climber," a colorful two-story sculpture. Kids take the stage in the Little Theater, create a computerized self-portrait, or build magnetic sculptures. The museum also features a climbing maze, crafts, and other exhibits to delight your younger family members. There's even a special area for five-and-unders.

In the summer, the museum is open Monday through Saturday 10:00 A.M. to 5:00 P.M. and Sunday from 1:00 to 5:00 P.M., and the rest of the year, Tuesday through Saturday 10:00 A.M. to 5:00 P.M. and Sunday noon to 5:00 P.M. Call (412) 322–5059 for admission prices and further information. Special educational programs and workshops are offered.

The sites of both **Fort Duquesne** and **Fort Pitt** are located in **Point State Park** in downtown Pittsburgh. Fort Duquesne was built by the French, Fort Pitt by the British. However, the British destroyed Fort Duquesne in 1758 and today, a bronze marker shows where that fort once stood. The British occupied Fort Pitt until 1772, when the Americans took over. You can see the **Fort Pitt Blockhouse** and the **Fort Pitt Museum,** plus enjoy the bonus of a park in the middle of a big city. Here you can view exhibits that describe Pittsburgh's early years.

"The Point" is where the Monongahela and Allegheny rivers come together to form the Ohio River. At the tip of the park you can see the fountain also known as "The Point."

Fort Pitt Museum is open in the winter Wednesday to Saturday 10:00 A.M. to 4:30 P.M., and Sunday noon to 4:30 P.M. In the summer, it is open Tuesday as well. Call (412) 281–9284.

NORTH SIDE

On the north side of Pittsburgh, you'll discover two wonderful attractions for families—the Carnegie Science Center and the National Aviary.

He's red, yellow, and blue, and he's got feathers. He's Zeke the Alien, host of children's programs at the world's most technologically sophisticated interactive planetarium, at the **Carnegie Science Center** (One Allegheny Avenue). You'll want to spend at least several hours here.

Science Spectacular is a must-see for all ages. This twenty-minute multimedia presentation teaches about cryogenics, robotics, electricity, and lasers—and it's a lot of fun. A laser beam activates a compact disc player, then as a ceiling fan rotates, the blades interrupt the beam. The music stops and starts again as the blade goes around, illustrating how lasers work. Amid the smoke and mirrors, you'll meet a talking robot and a real industrial robot arm, and you'll learn a lot.

Ports of Discovery comprises three exhibits aimed at kids. Children ages three to six can roll up their sleeves and literally get their hands wet in Early Learners' Landing. Kids can operate miniature paddlewheels, play with magnets, and pat a frog.

Science Pier is aimed at children seven to thirteen. Here, kids will gape at the holograms that demonstrate what lasers can do, look through a large microscope (Wentzscope), and observe a real living beehive. The Aquarium exhibit displays more than one hundred species of colorful fish. Kids can even board a real World War II submarine where, on weekends, you can see how the sub's communication system works. And Aquabatics is a two-story-tall interactive water sculpture that has to be experienced to be believed.

From Thanksgiving through April of every year, you can visit Pittsburgh's famous Great Miniature Railroad and Village. This replica of western Pennsylvania of the 1920s includes a minute ferris wheel, a circus parade, and real smoke puffing out of the steel mill.

The Science Center also has a four-story-tall Omnimax Theater where you feel as if you're a part of the movie action. Teenagers and college kids will want to put on modern 3-D glasses (not the old-fashioned red and green kind) and immerse themselves in a laser rock show.

The Science Center is open Monday through Thursday 10:00 A.M. to 5:00 P.M., Friday to Sunday 10:00 A.M. to 6:00 P.M. In the summer the center is open daily 10:00 A.M. to 6:00 P.M. The Omnimax Theater also has showings at 7:00 and 8:00 P.M. Friday and Saturday. Laser-rock music shows are also held "Late Nights" on Friday and Saturday. Call for titles and times. Hours also change for holidays. Tickets can be purchased separately for the exhibits, Omnimax, laser shows, and the submarine, or you may select from two different "combo" tickets. For information, call (412) 237–3400. Handicapped-accessible.

There are 450 live birds, many of them endangered, at the **National Aviary in Pittsburgh** (Allegheny Commons West), the largest free-standing indoor aviary in North America. In 1993 President Clinton designated this institution the National Aviary.

You'll see birds of all sizes and colors, from a tiny ruby-throated hummingbird to an Andean condor with a 10-foot wingspan, and more, including America's only pair of blue-winged kookaburras. The aviary itself presents a lush green indoor oasis, with no glass between you and the birds' habitats. A new Victorian-style dome is currently under construction, to span the entrance and educational center. A free parking lot will also be added, and more expansions are in the planning stages.

Open 9:00 A.M. to 4:30 P.M. seven days per week. Admission to the Aviary is $4.00 for adults, $3.00 for seniors, $2.50 for children two to twelve. Guided tours by reservation. Call (412) 323–7235 or 321–IFLY. Educational programs are available for children and adults, and new interactive displays are offered.

Artist and pop-icon Andy Warhol was born in Pittsburgh. Opened in 1994, the **Andy Warhol Museum** (located at 117 Sandusky Street on Pittsburgh's north side near the cultural district) is the largest single-artist museum in the world. Housed in a funky historic industrial warehouse are 1,000 paintings, drawings, prints, films, and a lot more. You can even get your picture taken Warhol-style. Call (412) 237–8300 for information about exhibitions of work by other contemporary artists and educational programs for children and adults. Open Wednesday and Sunday 11:00 A.M. to 6:00 P.M., Thursday through Saturday 11:00 A.M. until 8:00 P.M., closed Mondays and legal holidays. Admission is $5.00 for adults, $4.00 for seniors, $3.00 for children and students.

If your kids think art is stuffy, here's the antidote. Take them to the **Mattress Factory** (500 Sampsonia Way), housed in an old mattress factory in the Mexican War streets section, near the Andy Warhol Museum. This one-of-a-kind museum of contemporary art specializes in installations that physically surround you. For example, kids especially are mesmerized by the magical light effects in three permanent installations by artist James Turrell. A new garden piece by Winifred Lutz allows kids (and adults) to crawl through tunnels, climb up stairs, even enjoy a picnic lunch right in the middle of an artwork. In an "apartment" designed by Alan Wexler, everything is moveable. The museum also offers temporary installations designed specifically for the site by artists-in-residence.

A student guide pamphlet is available to help your family make the most of this experience with the playfulness of art. Call (412) 231–3169 for information. Open Tuesday to Saturday 10:00 A.M. to 5:00 P.M., Sunday 1:00 to 5:00 P.M. Handicapped-accessible. Admission is free.

THE "STRIP DISTRICT"

Pittsburgh's "strip district" has nothing to do with exotic dancing. This is the nickname given to Pittsburgh's open-air marketplace. It's fun to take in the atmosphere on this half-mile "strip" along Penn Avenue and Smallman Street, starting at Eleventh Street. Enjoy the colorful produce, the smells of ethnic food, bakeries, and restaurants, and other shops.

Near the strip district, give your children a really extraordinary experience by participating in a children's workshop at the **Society for Contemporary Crafts.**

Here, your family can both appreciate and participate in crafts together. The exhibition gallery mounts four temporary craft exhibitions per year. Meanwhile, in the children's studio, parents and kids can learn first-hand the techniques used by the artists. The children's studio offers an opportunity to work on an artist-designed project that corresponds to the current exhibition. For example, a recent exhibition called "Storytellers: Threads" focused on fiber arts such as embroidery and beadwork. In the children's studio, kids told their own stories with bits of fabric, yarn, thread, and buttons.

The studio is open whenever the Society is open, no reservations needed, and it's free to the public. Craft projects are open to all ages from the youngest child who can barely hold a pencil to great-grandparents. Come as you are and stay until your masterpiece is complete. The Society is open Tuesday through Saturday 10:00 A.M. to 5:00 P.M. Call (412) 261–7003 for more information.

The **Senator John Heinz Pittsburgh Regional History Center** (412–338–9006), scheduled to open in late April 1996, will feature permanent exhibits spotlighting life in Western Pennsylvania from 1750 to the present. It is planned to include a Children's Discovery Hall where hands-on exhibits will help children understand how history is researched, studied, and discovered.

Admission is $5.75 for adults, $4.25 for children ages three to eighteen and for seniors (age sixty-five and older). The museum will be open from 9:00 A.M. to 5:00 P.M. Wednesdays through Saturday and 11:00 A.M. to 5:00 P.M. on Sunday. It will also include a cafe and museum shop.

SOUTH SIDE

On the south side of Pittsburgh, you'll have an excellent opportunity to see the city from the water or from one of two inclines.

Board the *Gateway Clipper* at **Station Square,** a five-minute stroll across the Smithfield Street Bridge from downtown Pittsburgh. Two contiguous railroad buildings have been beautifully restored to create Station Square, a collection of sixty-five shops, eleven restaurants, and a hotel.

The **Gateway Clipper Fleet** (9 Station Square Dock) has a schedule of day and night cruises year-round ranging from narrated sightseeing trips to elegant dinner cruises with entertainment. Some cruises are aimed at children, such as the Goodship Lollypop Ride. All the riverboats are climate-controlled. Call (412) 355–7980 for information and a schedule of cruises.

Two of Pittsburgh's famous inclines are located nearby: the Monongahela Incline and the Duquesne Incline.

So what is an "incline" anyway? It's a cable railway designed to carry passengers or freight up Pittsburgh's steep hills. Inclines were invented before electric streetcars and before automobiles. Once, the city had seventeen of these engineering marvels. Today two survive, although now they are driven by electricity instead of the original steam. Thousands of commuters use the inclines every day. (Both stations and inclines are now wheelchair-accessible.)

The **Duquesne Incline** (1220 Grandview Avenue) has been in operation since 1877. The interiors are made of hand-carved cherry panels with oak and bird's-eye maple trim and amber glass transoms. For $1.00 each way, you can rise up 400 feet at a 30-degree angle to the New Observation Deck at the Upper Station and take in the spectacular vista. The incline operates Monday through Saturday 5:30 A.M. to 12:45 A.M., Sunday 7:00 A.M. to 12:45 A.M. Call (412) 381–1665 for information. Free parking is available at the Lower Station.

Across the street from Station Square is the **Monongahela Incline.** The "Mon," the first passenger incline is the United States, is 635 feet long and rises an elevation of about 368 feet at a 35-degree angle. The Mon runs Monday through Saturday 5:30 A.M. to 12:45 A.M. On Sundays and holidays it is open 8:45 A.M. to midnight. The fare is $1.00 each way. Call (412) 442–2000 for details.

What's the difference between the two? Well, the Duquesne has red cars and the tracks are lit with red lights. The Mon has green and yellow lights on the tracks, and the cares are ivory with black trim. Both have overlooks from Mount Washington, with a great view of the city. Both have historical information in their Upper Stations. The Duquesne's Upper Station is right on Restaurant Row (Grandview Avenue, well-named), so you can ride up and dine at one of Pittsburgh's best restaurants.

EAST PITTSBURGH

Three miles east of downtown you'll discover Pittsburgh's Oakland cultural district, where you can see the University of Pittsburgh, Carnegie-Mellon University, the Carnegie Museums of Art and Natural History, Schenley Park, and the Phipps

From Pittsburgh's Duquesne Incline, you'll have a spectacular view of the city. (Photo © Mark W. McNally)

Conservatory. Also in this area you can visit Kennywood Park, Sandcastle Waterpark, and the Pittsburgh Zoo. (Technically, Kennywood is in West Mifflin and Sandcastle is in West Hempstead, both of which are east of the city, so it gets a little confusing. In this guide, we have listed them under West Mifflin and West Hempstead respectively.)

Located on Forbes Avenue along with its neighbor, the Carnegie Museum of Art, the **Carnegie Museum of Natural History** (4400 Forbes Avenue) has one of the world's finest dinosaur collections, a hall of gems and minerals, Egyptian artifacts (including mummies), and "Polar World."

The dinosaur collection has full skeletons of eleven different species of dinosaur, including the ever-popular T. Rex. The Hillman Hall of Minerals and Gems includes some of the finest specimens of their kind, plus a dazzling display of fluorescent minerals. Polar World explores the culture of the Inuit, including their keenly observed carvings. There are also Egyptian artifacts, Native American artifacts, eleven million species of insects, butterflies, birds, and so much more.

The "Discovery Room," aimed at children under twelve, is open selected hours. There are also special programs for children including the Natural Science Academy Summer Camp.

Founded in 1896 by Andrew Carnegie, the **Carnegie Museum of Art** was planned as a collection of "the old masters of tomorrow." At that time, that meant artists like Winslow Homer, James McNeill Whistler, and Camille Pisarro. Today the museum is known for its collections of American, French Impressionist and Post-Impressionist works. It also includes European and American decorative arts, Asian and African art, and a new architectural department.

Schoolchildren will get a kick out of the Hall of Sculpture, patterned after a real Greek temple. Family, youth, and children's programs are available.

Since the Museum of Natural History and the Museum of Art are attached, one admission gets you into both, and there are often joint programs such as tours of both facilities. A special family program such as "Bug-Out" is sometimes available. In "Bug-Out," families go on self-guided tours at their own pace through both museums, "collecting" representations of insects in science and art. At the culmination, you create your very own bug. Call (412) 622–3328 for information.

Both museums are open Tuesday through Saturday 10:00 A.M. to 5:00 P.M., Sunday 1:00 to 5:00 P.M., closed on Mondays. Admission for adults is $5.00, seniors $4.00, children and students $3.00. Handicapped-accessible. Also adjacent you'll find the **Carnegie Music Hall** and the **Carnegie Library of Pittsburgh.**

Just across Forbes Avenue from the Carnegie is the **Stephen Foster Memorial** (Forbes Avenue at the Cathedral of Learning), where performances often take place, and where you can see a collection of memorabilia reflecting the life of the popular composer. Open weekdays 9:00 A.M. to 4:30 P.M.

Within a few steps of the Stephen Foster Memorial towers the University of Pittsburgh's **Cathedral of Learning.** Compare New England Colonial architectural style with French Empire, Russian Byzantine, Chinese Empire, Israeli, or Irish Romanesque. Twenty-three different nations are represented in the **Nationality Rooms Tours.** Funded by gifts from some of Pittsburgh's ethnic communities, the Nationality Rooms are functioning classrooms in which your family can tour "around the world" with a University student guide who has been trained to adapt the tour to different ages and interests. It is recommended that you make your reservations in advance. Tour fees are nominal: adults, $2.00; seniors $1.00; children over eight 50 cents. For tour information, call (412) 624–6000.

Also at the Cathedral of Learning, the stained-glass windows at the **Heinz Memorial Chapel** set a tone of Gothic other-worldliness. Call (412) 624–4157. Open 9:00 A.M. to 4:00 P.M. on weekdays. Mass is celebrated at noon every day. Services are also offered on Sundays, when the chapel is open 1:30 to 5:30 P.M.

Inside the Victorian glass structure of the **Phipps Conservatory** (located

FAITH AND EMILY'S FAVORITE ATTRACTIONS IN THE PITTSBURGH REGION

Kennywood Park
Sandcastle Park
Carnegie Science Center
Pittsburgh Children's Museum
Carnegie Museums of Art and Natural History
Duquesne or Monongahela Incline
Pittsburgh Zoo
Gateway Clipper
National Trolley Museum
Children's Studio at Society for Contemporary Crafts

in Schenley Park), you can see hundreds of orchids, palms, ferns, and other plants. The Japanese Courtyard Garden has an excellent collection of bonsai. The conservatory is the legacy of another of Pittsburgh's wealthy benefactors. Open year-round, Tuesday through Sunday 9:00 A.M. to 5:00 P.M. Outdoor gardens are open dawn to dusk at no charge. In the winter the indoor gardens soothe your cabin fever, and in warm weather you can enjoy both indoor and outdoor gardens, fountains, and glades. Call (412) 622–6914 for details.

The **Rodef Shalom Biblical Botanical Garden,** at Rodef Shalom Congregation, 4905 Fifth Avenue between Morewood and Devonshire, presents an unusual experience. This is the only biblical botanical garden in the state, and one of only a few in the country. Sunday School students can get a real picture of the Holy Land in this lovely setting where a spring literally flows in the desert. You can see olives, dates, pomegranates, cedars, lotus, papyrus, and bulrushes like the ones in which the pharaoh's daughter found Baby Moses.

Guided tours are available on selected Wednesdays. You can bring a brown-bag lunch. Although the garden is part of an active Jewish congregation, special programs are aimed at adults and children of both Jewish and Christian communities. A spectacular Sukkah is erected in the fall. Open at no charge from June 1 to September 15, Sunday through Thursday 10:00 A.M. to 2:00 P.M., Wednesday evenings from June through August 7:00 to 9:00 P.M. and on Saturdays from noon to 1:00 P.M. For further details, call (412) 621–6566.

Another one of Pittsburgh's leading citizens was Henry Clay Frick, who lived at **Clayton** until 1905 when he moved to New York City (where his next house also became a favorite museum). The **Frick Art and History Center,** 7227 Reynolds Street, (412) 238–9701, is a six-acre site that includes Clayton, the Frick Art Museum, historic Carriage Museum, Visitor Center, and cafe. The Victorian home has been meticulously restored and about 95 percent of the furnishings are original. The Carriage Museum displays old-fashioned automobiles, sleighs, and carriages. Little ones will be interested in the Visitor Center, which was once the playhouse of Helen, the Fricks' daughter. Free admission to most attractions, $5.00 general admission to the home.

Kids can scramble through a kid-sized replica of a naked mole rat tunnel in the brand-new children's zoo at the **Pittsburgh Zoo.** (If you've never seen a naked mole rat, you're in for a treat.) In "Kids Kingdom," moms and dads can relax on the patio while the kids learn to swing like spiders, slide like penguins, and enjoy the playground and the live animals. And just wait until your preschoolers try the new "Turtle Racers" ride.

The animals here have natural enclosures. Highlights include the Siberian tigers in the Asian Forest; lions, leopards, rhinos, elephants, gazelles of the African Savannah; and family groups of lowland gorillas, plus monkeys, gibbons, and orangutans of the Tropical Forest.

The zoo is located in Highland Park, ten minutes from downtown Pittsburgh. It's open daily except December 25. In the winter, the gates are open 9:00 A.M. to 4:00 P.M. If you're already inside the gate, you can stay until 5:00 P.M. In the summertime, the gates open at 10:00 A.M. and close at 5:00 P.M., and you can stay inside until 6:00 P.M. Parking is $2.50 per vehicle. Admission is $6.00 for adults, $4.00 for seniors sixty and over, $4.00 for children two to thirteen.

Also in the neighborhood, baseball fans can visit the remains of **Forbes Field,** including Mazeroski's Wall.

Pittsburgh is also a great sports town. The **Civic Arena** is home to the Pittsburgh Penguins (ice hockey), Stingers (roller hockey), and Phantoms (indoor soccer). For information on these three sports call (412) 642–1300. For other events at the Civic Arena, such as WWF Wrestling, call (412) 323–1919. **Three Rivers Stadium** is where the Pirates (baseball) and Steelers (football) play. For credit card ticket sales, call the Civic Arena at (412) 333–7328. There is no general information number for Three Rivers Stadium, but for the Pirates, call (412) 323–5000, and for the Steelers, call (412) 323–1200 (however, the Steelers are perpetually sold out).

While in Pittsburgh, you may wish to take in a performance at one of the many cultural venues: **Heinz Hall for the Performing Arts** (600 Penn

Avenue, 412–392–4909); **Civic Light Opera** (Benedum Center, 719 Liberty Avenue, 412–281–3973); **Coca-Cola Star Lake Amphitheater** (Route 18, at Route 22, 412–947–7400); **The Playhouse** (222 Craft Avenue, 412–621–6695); **Mendelssohn Choir of Pittsburgh** (P.O. Box 334, Pittsburgh 15230, 412–561–3353); **Pittsburgh Center for the Arts** (6300 Fifth Avenue, 412–361–0873); or **Pittsburgh Opera** (711 Penn Avenue, 412–281–0912).

WEST MIFFLIN

Memories of a childhood in Pittsburgh usually include scrambling around a rocking Noah's Ark in **Kennywood Park** (4800 Kennywood Boulevard in West Mifflin). Voted "Favorite Amusement Park" for nine years in a row by the National Amusement Park Historical Association (NAPHA), Kennywood Park has also been called the "Roller Coaster Capital of the World." Kennywood's Thunderbolt was recently named NAPHA's second favorite wood roller coaster, and its Steel Phantom NAPHA's third favorite steel coaster. And if all that isn't reason enough to visit the park, it has also been said that Kennywood's french fries are the best in the world.

A Pittsburgh landmark since 1898, today Kennywood is also a National

Voted "Favorite Amusement Park" for nine years in a row by the National Amusement Park Historical Association, Kennywood is a great place for making memories. (Courtesy Kennywood Park)

Historic Landmark. The carousel pavilion and a restaurant are the original structures. Others were added over the years. One roller coaster, for example, the Jack Rabbit, with its "camel back" (double dip) looks just the way it did in 1921. "Pittsburg's Lost Kennywood" re-creates Luna parks of the past. But Kennywood Park has continued to evolve, with the new Laser Loop, Steel Phantom, and other new features.

Kennywood makes your visit easy on your wallet in several ways. First, you're welcome to bring along a cooler and eat in the picnic grove. Another unique feature is the pricing schedule. Kennywood offers both a Ride-All-Day ticket that includes everything and a general admission. General admission, only $4.50 for adults and children older than three ($3.50 for seniors!), can be a bargain for anyone who doesn't plan to go on many rides but still wishes to accompany the family. This ticket lets you into the park but you have to pay for any rides separately. These two features allow families to save a little money and still have a great time together.

Prices vary seasonally, but in general on weekdays you can get a ride-all-day ticket for $15.00, and on weekends for $18.00.

Kennywood is only minutes away from downtown Pittsburgh, off the Swissdale exit (Exit 9) of Interstate 376 (Penn-Lincoln Parkway). Although some rides will get you wet, none require bathing suits. Open daily mid-May through Labor Day noon to 10:00 P.M. Call (412) 461–0500.

WEST HOMESTEAD

Sandcastle Action Park, Kennywood's sister park at 1000 Sandcastle Drive in West Homestead, began life as an abandoned steel mill and was opened as a water park in July 1990. Sandcastle is a major riverside water park with a boardwalk, fifteen water slides, two pools, and a Lazy River. It also has two race car tracks, video games, and miniature golf.

Only the bravest water-sliders should attempt the Lightning Express twin body slides, 60 feet high and 250 feet long, each with a double dip, followed by a monster free fall. (AAAH!)

Another slide, Cliffhangers, uses a new concept in water slide design: sky ponds. Each pond is at a different level above the ground. You and your inner tube can float in one pond before sliding down to the next. If that doesn't sound like your speed, relax on the Lazy River with its whirlpools, fountains, and gentle current.

Sandcastle is located in West Homestead, five minutes from the Squirrel Hill Tunnel, between the Homestead High Level and Glenwood bridges on Pennsylvania Route 837. Call (412) 462–6666 for details.

Open daily in season, usually June through Labor Day weekend, 11:00

A.M. to 6:00 P.M. The park stays open until 7:00 P.M. in July and August. Admission prices: Slide-All-Day $13.95 for adults and children three and older (includes all water activities—hot tubs, pools, Lazy River, and fifteen water slides); pool pass (includes everything except water slides) $7.95; senior citizen pool pass $4.95. Parking and boat docking are free. Special events and festivals are held in Sandcastle's Riverplex entertainment complex.

SPRINGDALE

Rachel Carson said, "Those who contemplate the beauty of the earth find reserves of strength that will endure as long as life lasts." The famous author of *Silent Spring* was born in 1907 in the farmhouse now known as the **Rachel Carson Homestead,** 613 Marion Avenue in Springdale, within minutes of Pittsburgh. As your family travels this region that is so much a part of our industrial development, a visit to Carson's home is a healthy reminder of the downside of "progress."

You can tour the nineteenth-century house and find out about one woman who made a difference. *Silent Spring* and Carson's other books pointed out for the first time the dangers of DDT and other pesticides. Her special interest in exposing children to nature was illustrated by her 1956 article "Help Your Child to Wonder." You'll also enjoy the gardens, especially the Butterfly Garden.

Open April through November, Saturday 11:00 A.M. to 4:00 P.M. and Sunday 1:00 to 5:00 P.M. At other times, you may call (412) 274–5459 for an appointment. Special children's programs are offered, such as Wonder Week, an environmental day camp in the summer. In May, Rachel Carson's birthday is celebrated and in October, the homestead is host to a family fall festival.

TARENTUM

You'll have to wear a miner's hard hat and mind your head as you board a mining car, modernized for comfort and electrically powered, to travel a half-mile underground at **Tour-Ed Mine and Museum** (Bull Creek Road at Exit 14 of Route 28 North; 412–224–4720) into a genuine coal mine. Your tour guide, a real miner, will help you learn about the history of coal mining. It's chilly down here, so bring your sweater. This is not for the claustrophobic.

You can also see the company store, 1785 log home, and sawmill. You can even see a bedroom set up like the ones where the miners slept. Located on the Allegheny Valley Expressway, only a few miles northeast of the Rachel Carson Homestead, opposite Woodlawn Golf Course. Open Wednesday to Monday, Memorial Day to Labor Day, 1:00 to 4:00 P.M. Admission is $6.00 for adults, $3.00 for children. The tour takes about two hours.

BUTLER

The Butler County Historical Society administers several historic sites in the county, including the new **Butler County Heritage Center** (119 West New Castle Street). This center, opened in 1995, presents temporary exhibits on the history of this area. On permanent display, you'll find artifacts from Butler county's many industries, including a tin shop, a Bantam jeep, Spang oil tools, Franklin glasswork, and farm tools.

Other sites administered by the Historical Society include: **Cooper Cabin** off Route 356 on Cooper Road; the **Senator Walter Lowrie (Shaw) House** at 123 Diamond Street; and the **Little Red School House Museum** at 200 East Jefferson Street. Families will be most attracted to the Little Red Schoolhouse and Cooper Cabin. For information, or to arrange a tour of the Historical Society's sites, call (412) 283–8116.

Last Halloween families gathered around a bonfire at Cooper Cabin to hear ghost stories. On weekends from April through October, the cabin offers demonstrations of horse-shoeing, basket-weaving quilting, spinning, and weaving, as well as an herb garden and outbuildings such as a spinning house, spring house and tool shed.

At the Little Red School House you sit down in a real old-fashioned desk as your tour guide transforms into a teacher. The school house was built in 1838.

AMBRIDGE

Old Economy Village (Fourteenth and Church streets in Ambridge) was built by the same Christian communal society who built Harmony (see page 103). Here you can visit seventeen restored buildings and gardens, and learn about how this unusual community lived. The Harmonists expected the Second Coming in 1829, so they lived celibate lives, always stored one year's supply of grain, and hoarded gold.

Your whole visit takes about an hour and a half including the orientation film, *Those Who Believed,* and tour of the exhibits, gardens, and buildings. The village had its own tailor, printer, shoemaker, cabinetmaker, locksmith, and more, and the village store still posts the 1927 price list. Kids will enjoy using the hand pump to pour themselves a drink.

Old Economy Village is 18 miles northwest of Pittsburgh on Route 65. Open Tuesday through Saturday 9:00 A.M. to 5:00 P.M., Sunday noon to 4:00 P.M. Closed winter holidays. Adults eighteen to sixty-four pay $5.00, seniors $4.00, children six to seventeen $3.00. Children under six are free. Many special events and tours are available, including educational programs and Candlelight Christmas. Call (412) 266–4500 for admission fees and information.

One of the largest and most beautiful state parks in Pennsylvania, **Raccoon Creek State Park** has about 7,000 acres and Raccoon Creek Lake, which itself is more than 100 acres.

Located in Raccoon Creek State Park, only steps east of the park entrance, is the 315-acre **Wildflower Reserve,** where you can choose between easy-walking trails and trails with gentle grades. Your best bet to see the most blooms is April or May, but something is blooming from late March through the summer. If you're lucky, you might see deer, raccoons, wild turkeys, mink, birds, and other wildlife. Trails are open year-round from 8:00 A.M. to sunset. Comfortable shoes are a must. On Soldier Days, you can view historic re-enactments, military displays, and more. For details, call (412) 899–3611.

The park is located in southern Beaver County, 25 miles west of Pittsburgh. Take Route 22 or Route 30. Access to the park is via Route 18. Recreational facilities include boating, hiking, camping, swimming, and picnicking. Modern family cabins are available year-round, with electric heat, kitchens, and toilets.

While you're in Raccoon Creek State Park, you may wish to visit **Frankfort Mineral Springs,** about one-half mile south of the park entrance. From the 1790s to 1932, this was the site of a popular spa where many were attracted to the purported medicinal properties of the spring water. Call (412) 899–2200.

NEW BRIGHTON

The **Lapic Winery, Ltd.** offers tours and wine-tastings seasonally. Located at 682 Tulip Drive, Daugherty Turnpike, off Route 68 in New Brighton. Hours vary seasonally, so check by calling (412) 846–2031.

The **Merrick Free Art Gallery** (Fifth Avenue at Eleventh Street) houses the collection of French, German, English, and American paintings of the eighteenth and nineteenth centuries that belonged to Edward Dempster Merrick. It has a display of artifacts belonging to the New Brighton Historical Society as well. The Gallery also mounts many special exhibits such as its annual Victorian Christmas Toy Show. Open Tuesday through Saturday 10:00 A.M. to 4:30 P.M. and Sunday 1:00 to 4:30 P.M. Call (412) 846–1130 for information.

HARMONY

The village of Harmony was founded in 1804 by members of a religious communal group, the Harmony Society. This group eventually built about 130 buildings including two outlying villages. Today, Harmony is known for its antiques shops, museums, restaurants, and parks.

The **Harmony Museum** (Mercer Street) offers walking tours of the historic district of Harmony, as well as the **Ziegler Log House** and the **Wagner House.** Tours are available June 1 to September 30, 1:00 to 4:00 P.M. daily except Monday. Admission is $2.50 for adults, $1.00 for children. Call (412) 452–7341. Open June to September, daily 1:00 to 4:00 P.M.; October to May, Monday, Wednesday, Friday, and Sunday 1:00 to 4:00 P.M. Closed holidays. Call (412) 452–7341 for information and admission prices. Limited handicapped accessibility.

ZELIENOPLE

Twenty-eight miles north of Pittsburgh on Route 19 is the historic town of Zelienople. The Zelienople Historical Society has restored the **Passavant House** and **Buhl House** (243 South Main Street and 221 South Main Street, respectively). Passavant House is primarily devoted to the furnishings and memorabilia of the Passavant family, who played an important role in the town's history. Buhl House displays a collection that tells the history of the entire community. Open May 1 to September 30, Wednesday and Saturday 1:00 to 4:00 P.M., otherwise by appointment. Call (412) 452–9457.

PORTERSVILLE

Moraine State Park (located at 225 Pleasant Valley Road, off Route 422 in Portersville) offers a great variety of family-oriented nature programs. For example, for children ages ten to fifteen there are fishing workshops that teach the Pennsylvania Fish and Boat Commission's guidelines for S.M.A.R.T. fishing (Safety, Manners, Appreciation, Release, and Teaching). There are nature walks and canoe trips. Having recently reintroduced ospreys to Lake Arthur, the park offers educational programs about these and other waterfowl. You can rent motorboats, pontoons, or sailboats. Call (412) 368–8811 for details.

Also administered by Moraine State Park is **McConnell's Mill State Park.** It's definitely worth the walk to see the 400-foot Slippery Rock Creek Gorge, formed by the glaciers thousands of years ago. The huge boulders literally "slipped" down the walls of the gorge, creating a strange and wonderful landscape. You can also explore the 2,500 acres of park land, have a picnic, hike one of the trails, or take a free guided tour. If you have your own boat, you can go kayaking or rafting. The grist mill is currently under restoration, and is open for free guided tours Memorial Day to Labor Day, 10:00 A.M. to 6:00 P.M. For more information and park hours, call (412) 368–8091.

Also located nearby, at 2951 Prospect Road, Slippery Rock, is the only

FAITH AND EMILY'S FAVORITE EVENTS IN THE PITTSBURGH REGION

"Streetcar Named Expire" (October) (412) 228–9256

"Fireworks Capital of the World" July Fourth Celebration in New Castle (412) 654–5593

Holidays at the Carnegie (November through December) (412) 622–3131

Great Miniature Railroad & Village, Carnegie Science Center (November through December) (412) 237–3400

Pittsburgh Children's Festival, Pittsburgh's North Side (mid-May) (412) 321–5520

environmental education center in western Pennsylvania, and one of only four in the state, the **Jennings Environmental Education Center.** This site is a true relict prairie ecosystem.

A what? A relict prairie ecosystem is a prairie formed by prehistoric glacial activity. Here, the glacier left only 4 to 6 inches of topsoil, with clay underneath. As a result, trees don't grow here, but grasses and windflowers do. If you visit in late July or August, you can see spectacular windflowers in bloom, such as the spiky purple blazing star. The prairie also supports unusual wildlife, such as the eastern massasauga rattlesnake, one of Pennsylvania's three species of poisonous snakes, and an endangered species in the state.

You can hike or picnic here from dawn to dusk, seven days a week. The Education Center is open Monday through Friday, 8:00 A.M. to 4:00 P.M. or whenever educational programs are offered. In the spring and summer, special programs highlight the wildflowers in bloom. In March you can learn about maple sugaring and in April Earth Day programs teach about biodiversity. Many other programs are also available. Call (412) 794–6011 for information about current educational programs.

NEW CASTLE

Bet you didn't know that New Castle, Pennsylvania, is the "Fireworks Capital of the World." Two of the largest fireworks manufacturers, Pyrotecnico and

Zambelli Internationale, are based in this city northwest of Pittsburgh.

So, if you happen to be in the area around the Fourth of July, check out the **Fireworks Festival** here. In 1995, the festivities included a special children's ground fireworks display in which kids were able to see the fireworks close-up. Another feature was "Locomotion," in which an antique locomotive came to life with fireworks, lights, and music. For details, contact the Lawrence County Tourist Promotion Agency, Shenango Street Station, 138 West Washington Street, New Castle 16101; (412) 654–5593; fax, (412) 654–3330.

Family-owned, family-operated, and family-friendly, **Harlansburg Station's Museum of Transportation** (routes 19 and 108) looks just like an old railroad station, with four Pennsylvania Railroad cars in front. Inside one of the cars you can see displays of railroad memorabilia such as uniforms, silver, linens, and more. As you enter the museum a model conductor greets you. Inside the museum you're surrounded by planes, trains, cars, and trucks—all kinds of transportation. There's a Ford Model T and Model A, an extensive collection of railroad lanterns, and a gift shop brimming with everything for the transportation buff.

The museum is open seasonally, so call (412) 652–9002 for current hours. Generally, the museum is open weekends only in March, April, November, and December, Saturday 10:00 A.M. to 5:00 P.M. and Sunday noon to 5:00 P.M. From May through October, it is open Tuesday through Saturday 10:00 A.M. to 5:00 P.M. and Sunday noon to 5:00 P.M. Closed Mondays, and January through February.

Two mansions once belonging to members of the Hoyt family now comprise the **Hoyt Institute of Fine Arts** (124 East Leasure Avenue). Self-guided tour brochures have recently become available for both "Hoyt West" (the Alex Crawford Hoyt Mansion) and "Hoyt East" (the May Emma Hoyt Mansion). Art from the permanent collection is on display at Hoyt West, while temporary exhibitions are generally held in Hoyt East, as are art classes for children and adults. Summer art camps are offered for children ages six to eight and nine to twelve. Open Tuesday to Saturday 9:00 A.M. to 4:00 P.M. Call (412) 652–2882 for admission prices. Partially handicapped-accessible.

Get up close to over one hundred species of friendly animals from all over the world at **Living Treasures Animal Park,** on Route 422. Open weekends 10:00 A.M. to 6:00 P.M. in May, September, and October, and daily 10:00 A.M. to 8:00 P.M. Memorial Day through Labor Day. Admission is $5.50 for adults, $4.50 for children two to twelve, and children under two are free. Call (412) 924–9571 for information.

VOLANT

Main Street in the quaint rural town of Volant offers more than fifty shops and restaurants featuring Victorian collectibles, arts and crafts, Christmas specialties, housewares, pottery, and special events such as a Quilt Show and Sale in July, an Autumn Pumpkin Festival, Old Fashioned Christmas, and more. Volant is located north of New Castle, on Route 208, ten minutes from routes I–79 and I–80. It is just minutes away from McConnell's Creek State Park and Living Treasures Animal Park. There's also a thriving Amish community in this area.

The shops are open daily except for New Year's Day, Easter, Thanksgiving, and Christmas. Hours are 10:00 A.M. to 5:00 P.M. Monday through Saturday, and noon to 5:00 P.M. on Sunday. For more information, call the Volant Merchants Association at (412) 533–2591.

AVELLA

Sixteen thousand years of history and pre-history in western Pennsylvania are brought to life at the **Meadowcroft Museum of Rural Life** (401 Meadowcroft Road). The grounds here include the archaeological site that contains the earliest evidence of human life in eastern North America. (This part of the site is not open to the public at this time, but displays explain about the work in progress.)

Tours here are designed to engage the entire family. Everyone can sit down in a one-room schoolhouse and take part in a real school lesson, reading from *McGuffey's Reader.* Then try some of the playground games children played 150 years ago. Learn about the daily lives of Native Americans, early European settlers, farmers, loggers, and coal miners. Explore log houses, a covered bridge, and a blacksmith's shop.

Located off Route 50, less than an hour from Pittsburgh, the museum offers many hands-on educational programs for groups. Gardeners will be especially interested in the museum's heirloom garden project. Wear good walking shoes, because the paths between the buildings are natural.

Open May through October Wednesday through Saturday 10:00 A.M. to 5:00 P.M., and Sunday 1:00 to 6:00 P.M. The last complete tour starts at 3:00 P.M. on Wednesday to Saturday, and at 4:00 P.M. on Sunday. Call (412) 587–3412 for information about admission prices, group reservations, and many special workshops.

WASHINGTON

The **Pennsylvania Trolley Museum,** One Museum Road (412–228–9256), is the only museum where you can see, learn about, and actually ride historic electric rail vehicles from Pittsburgh, Philadelphia, Johnstown, and other cities. Take several generations along for an opportunity for reminiscing and inter-generational storytelling.

First, go to the brand-new Visitor Education Center to buy your tickets and view an exhibit. Stop and browse through the exhibits, or take in a film. During the winter holidays, you can even find yourself at the controls of a model train layout.

Rides leave from the Richfor shelter across the picnic area and next to the car barn. You just won't believe how beautifully these streetcars have been restored. Your motorman, and the entire staff (except the director), are enthusiastic volunteers. You'll clatter on a 3-mile journey past a scenic section that was once an old coal-mining railroad. After you climb off the trolley, you may view about twenty-five trolley cars from the museum's collection, including the real "Streetcar Named Desire" from New Orleans. You can even peek in on the car shop where volunteers restore the cars. Bring along a picnic lunch if you like.

Just 30 miles southwest of Pittsburgh, near Exit 8 (Meadow Lands) off I–79, the Trolley Museum is convenient to Meadowcroft Village in Avella. Open noon to 5:00 P.M. daily during July and August, and weekends noon to 5:00 P.M. in May, June, September, October, and December. Admission is $5.00 for adults, $4.00 for seniors sixty-five and over, and $3.00 for children two to eleven. Special events include: a Trolley Fair in June, with a trolley parade, antique vehicle display, and hand car and caboose rides; the spooky "Streetcar Named Expire" for Halloween; and "Santa Trolley" in December.

Washington County Historical Society's LeMoyne House (49 East Maiden Street) houses the headquarters of the Washington County Historical Society, including its collection of Civil War weapons and a time capsule prepared by President Ulysses S. Grant. The beautiful stone home also served as Dr. LeMoyne's medical office and still contains some of his old medical instruments and books. It was also a stop on the Underground Railroad.

Call (412) 225–6740 for admission prices. Open February to mid-December, Wednesday to Friday noon to 4:00 P.M. and Sunday 2:00 to 4:00 P.M.

NORTHEASTERN PENNSYLVANIA

With the Delaware and Susquehanna rivers, the Pocono Mountains, wilderness areas, numerous lakes, and crystal clear rivers, Northeastern Pennsylvania has attracted vacationers since the 1800s. But Northeastern Pennsylvania is more than just a resort area. The discovery of one of the world's largest deposits of anthracite coal made the region a center for industry. Entrepeneurs, immigrant workers, and others came to the area to make money or find work. The country's first railroads were built to transport the coal to the cities. Other industries moved their operations here to take advantage of the cheap fuel.

Thanks to its history—both natural and industrial—northeastern Pennsylvania offers a special mix to family vacationers today. Those looking for hiking, skiing, boating, and relaxing resorts will not be disappointed. But the region's industrial history adds some more unusual attractions, such as factories, railroad excursions, and coal mine tours.

DELAWARE WATER GAP

For those arriving in Pennsylvania from New Jersey, the Delaware Water Gap serves as a gateway to the Poconos. This natural land formation along the Kittatiny Ridge is a dramatic backdrop for hiking, canoeing, or biking. The

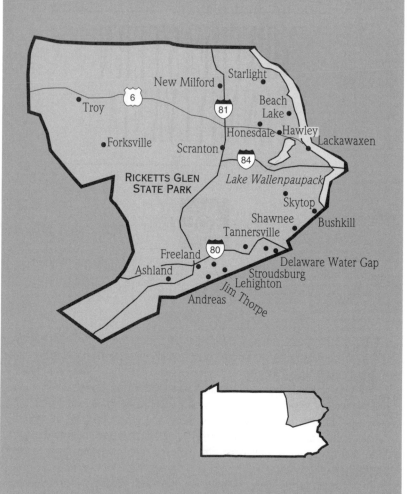

New Milford
Starlight
Troy
6
81
Beach
Lake
Forksville
Honesdale
Hawley
Lackawaxen
Scranton
84
RICKETTS GLEN
STATE PARK
Lake Wallenpaupack
Skytop
Shawnee
Bushkill
Tannersville
Freeland
80
Delaware Water Gap
Ashland
Stroudsburg
Lehighton
Andreas
Jim Thorpe

Northeastern Pennsylvania

Delaware Water Gap National Recreation Area (headquartered in Bushkill; 717–588–6637) extends from the Delaware Water Gap (the town and site) to Milford, 37 miles to the north. There are several canoe and rafting liveries along the river. Try Kittatinny Canoes in Dingmans Ferry (800–FLOATKC), Adventure Sports in Marshalls Creek (800–487–2628), Chamberlain Canoes in Minisink Mills (800–422–6631), or Shawnee Canoe Trips in Shawnee-on-Delaware (800–SHAWNEE). These companies offer different excursions, ranging from a couple of hours to all day. The Delaware is generally a pretty calm river, but there are some rapids along the way. Be sure to specify your family members' ages and abilities when deciding which excursion is best for you. Another way to explore the Water Gap is on the **Delaware Water Gap Trolley** (717–476–0010) which takes vacationers from the depot on Route 611 near the town's center. There's great hiking in the area—the Appalachian trail cuts through at the Water Gap—with some shorter trails that even little legs can handle without problems.

SHAWNEE-ON-DELAWARE

The river is great for boating, but kids will enjoy swimming and sliding at **Shawnee Place Play and Water Park** (717–721–7231), located just north of Route 80 (take Exit 52 to Route 209 and follow signs). Especially geared for smaller children, the park has two slides and two pools, both about 3 feet deep. There are three magic shows daily as well as chair lift rides and other attractions. Entry is $10.00 each for adults or children. For those who want to watch but not get wet, there's a $5.00 spectator fee that allows you into the magic shows and chair lift but not on the water rides. Open daily 10:00 A.M. to 5:00 P.M. Memorial Day through Labor Day weekends.

In the winter, **Shawnee Mountain**—with twenty-three trails, a snowboarding area and a vertical drop of 700 feet—has an extensive ski program for kids. There's a Ski Wee program for five- to twelve-year-olds. Little ones (three to five years) can join the Pre-Ski Wee group. And more adventurous kids ages ten to fifteen will want to hook up with the Mountain Cruisers. Programs start at $50 a day or $35 for a half-day. Three- and five-day packages are available. For non-skiing children, the Little Wigwam Children's Center is open daily for babysitting 9:00 A.M. to 5:00 P.M. on weekdays and 8:00 A.M. to 5:00 P.M. on weekends.

BUSHKILL

In the town of Bushkill, check out two museums located on either side of Route 209. The **Mary Stoltz Doll Museum** (717–588–7566) is definitely a don't-touch place, but, if you have a doll lover in the family, the collection of 125 dolls makes it well worth resisting the temptation. Across the street, the **Pocono Indian Museum** (717–588–9338) explores the history of the Delaware Indians.

Continuing up Route 209, you'll reach **Bushkill Falls** (717–588–6682), billed as the Niagara Falls of Pennsylvania. The Peters family started charging admission to see the eight magnificent falls on their 300 acres back in 1905. The tourists haven't stopped coming since. Take a short nature walk back to the falls. Small children can usually manage the easy forty-five-minute to one-hour stroll. For the more energetic, there's a 2-mile hike that affords an even better view. Bushkill Falls is open April through November from 9:00 A.M. to dusk. Admission is $7.00 for adults; $2.00 for children ages four to ten.

STROUDSBURG

Take a trip back in time at the **Quiet Valley Living Historical Farm,** off Route 209 southwest of Stroudsburg. Here your family will spend time with the Zeppers, a German immigrant family that settled this land back in 1765.

After a brief welcoming presentation, you'll say goodbye to the 1990s, and step back into the 1800s. In the kitchen, you will learn how food is prepared and nothing is wasted on the farm. The daughters will show you their dowry chests and demonstrate how they help out around the house. And the farm hand will introduce you to the animals, demonstrate the farm equipment, and let your kids jump into the hay pile.

The museum is open daily from the end of June until Labor Day. Monday through Saturday the hours are 9:30 A.M. to 5:30 P.M., Sunday, 1:00 to 5:30 P.M. Admission is charged. The museum also has special holiday presentations, with a Harvest Festival in October and an Old Time Christmas celebration in December. Call (717) 992–6161 for more information and specific dates.

TANNERSVILLE

Continuing west on Route 80, the **Camelback Ski Area** (717–629–1661) is worth a stop in any season. In the winter, Camelback is one of the Pocono's largest ski resorts with more than thirty trails, twelve lifts, and a vertical drop of 800 feet. There's a full-scale ski program where children ages four to nine can spend the day learning to ski. Each day includes at least three hours of ski instruction and continuous supervision from 9:00 A.M. to 3:30 P.M. The fee is $50 for a half day; $65 for a full day, including lift ticket. Special three- and five-day packages are available. For little ones too young for the slopes, babysitting is available during the day.

From May until the end of fall, Camelback transforms from a ski resort

During summer, Camelback Ski Resort attracts family vacationers with fun sports and activities, such as miniature golf. (Courtesy Martin Livezey)

to a family recreation area, with miniature golf, kiddie cars, Alpine slide, and a slew of water games and rides. Ride the chair lift to the top of the mountain and hike down, taking in the view of the Pocono Mountains. Buy a combo ticket ($19.95 per person, discounted after Labor Day) and ride and play all day. There's also a summer day camp program at the facility and kids ages five to twelve can sign up for a day, a week, or the whole summer. A two-day vacationer package is about $60.

SKYTOP

When we were children, our parents took us to several resorts within a couple hours of our home in New York. Although some were by the ocean, others in the mountains, all had a few elements in common: a stately lodge, a rocking-chair porch, great trails for hiking and walking, and a casual but classy approach to everything.

Skytop Lodge, on Route 390 north of Tannersville, was one of those places—and it hasn't changed much in the intervening years. Rather than a resort that caters to kids, Skytop accommodates families the same way it accommodates all its guests: with individual attention and concern for detail. Families can check into Skytop for a weekend or a week and find plenty to do for everyone: hiking and cross-country ski trails from 1 mile to 10; guided nature walks and self-guided fitness trails; mountain bikes, rowboats, and canoes available on site; a swimming lake and indoor and outdoor pools; a game room; and a gorgeous golf course. Downhill skiing is just minutes away.

Skytop offers Camp in the Clouds for children ages three to twelve every day in summer and weekends year-round. The program, which runs from 9:30 A.M. to 4:00 P.M., includes arts and crafts, nature walks, swimming, and other supervised activities. The cost is $14 per day per child.

Skytop is a splurge; but if you can swing it, it's an excellent family vacation. Accommodations are on the American plan, which means all meals are included. The menu includes some excellent entrées for adults and some favorites for kids. Rates run from $240 to $370 per room per night weekdays; $260 to $395 on weekends. There is a $15-per-day charge for children seventeen and under who stay in their parents' room. For more information, call Skytop at (800) 345–7759.

HAWLEY–LAKE WALLENPAUPACK

On your way north on 390 from Skytop, you'll pass through **Promised Land State Park,** a 3,000-acre park surrounded by state forest land for a total of 11,000 acres of wilderness. The area is home to a wide variety of wildlife, including one of eastern Pennsylvania's bigger populations of black bear. There are numerous housekeeping cabin resorts along Route 390 and camping is available in the park. Twenty five miles of trails, 535 campsites in four areas, two lakes, and plenty of picnic areas make this a great place for family adventures. Boats are available for rent in the park. There are environmental programs for children during the summer. The three primitive campgrounds are open year-round for cross-country skiers who can't bear to go home at the end of the day. Call (717) 676–3428 or (800) 63PARKS for more information.

If you're in the area during winter, check out nearby **Tanglewood Ski Resort,** which offers nine trails of downhill skiing, a snowboarding area, and several cross-country ski trails. There's a Ski Wee children's program and nursery available for small children. The ski shop is one of the only ones in the area to rent cross-country equipment as well as downhill. For more information call (717) 226–9500.

Continuing north from Tanglewood on Route 6, you'll find **Lake Wallenpaupack,** the state's third largest man-made lake: 15 miles long with 52 miles of shoreline. It was created in the 1920s by Pennsylvania Power & Light (PP&L) as part of a major hydroelectric project. At the **PP&L Visitor's Center** on Route 6 south of Hawley, exhibits outline the development of the project as well as available recreation on and around the lake. While there, ask about **Shuman**

FAITH AND EMILY'S FAVORITE ATTRACTIONS IN NORTHEASTERN PENNSYLVANIA

Float trip on the Delaware River, Delaware Water Gap and
  Lackawaxen
Mountain Biking in the Lehigh Gorge, Jim Thorpe
Skytop Lodge, Skytop
World's End State Park, Forksville
Lackawanna Coal Mine Tour, Scranton
Woodloch Pines Inn and Resort, Hawley

Point, and **Ledgedale** natural area, and **Beech House Creek Wildlife Refuge,** all maintained for public use by PP&L. They are great places for short nature hikes and spotting wildlife such as beavers, herons, hawks, and more.

Along the lake there are numerous resorts and marinas geared to vacationers who want to spend time on the water. Rent a powerboat for the day at **Club Nautico of Lake Wallenpaupack,** located at Shepards Marina on Route 507 (717–226–0580). A wide variety of brand new and meticulously maintained powerboats and Waverunners are available, as is equipment for waterskiing, tubing, and other sports. If you don't have boating experience, ask for a list of skippers available for hire.

Other outfitters that rent boats on the lake include the **Pine Crest Yacht Club, Inc.,** also on Route 507 (717–857–1136; sail-, row-, fishing, and water-skiing boats available) and **Pocono Action Sports** (717–857–1976).

For a sunset dinner cruise or a one-hour sightseeing tour on the lake, the 48-foot *Spirit of Paupack* is a great way to see the lake. Call for current rates and schedules: (717) 857–1251.

On the opposite side of the lake, off Route 590 near Hamlin, **Claws 'n' Paws Wild Animal Park** is a unique private zoo with more than one hundred species of animals. There's a petting area with fawns and kids and other baby animals. The zoo recently acquired a rare snow leopard and a white tiger. There are also bears, otters, primates of several types, alligators, and many species of birds. The easy-to-follow trails through the woods and the size of the facility help younger children from getting overwhelmed and overtired by the experience.

Admission is $7.95 for adults, $4.95 for children two to eleven. The park is open daily from the beginning of May to the end of October, 10:00 A.M. to 6:00 P.M. Call 717-698-6154 for more information.

Off Route 590 heading toward the town of Hawley, you'll see signs to the **Triple "W" Riding Stables,** a 171-acre horse ranch that features western riding experiences. The staff at Triple W ensure a fun and rewarding ride for all members of the family by taking into consideration level of expertise and ambition. Overnight camping on horseback, hayrides, and sleigh rides are also available. Riding rates for a family of four start at $26 per person per hour. The overnight camping trip is $105 per person. Call for more information and reservations: (717) 226–2620.

If you follow 590 East from Hawley, you'll arrive at an excellent family resort, **Woodloch Pines Inn & Resort.** Named three times by *Better Homes & Gardens* magazine as one of America's favorite family vacation resorts, Woodloch Pines was established as a small inn back in 1958. Since then, it's grown into a complex with 160 hotel rooms, a dinner theater, several restaurants, game rooms, and more family activities and children's programs than you can cram into a seven-day stay.

The resort is located right on Lake Teedyuskung, sixty-five acres of crystal-clear waters with a sandy swimming beach and rowboats for exploring on your own. Woodloch Pines has the space and the layout that allow some families to be quiet and relax with each other while other groups applaud and cheer each other in games and contests.

Woodloch Pines rates include three meals a day and all activities and rentals. For families who prefer a more independent vacation, homes are available for rent at Woodloch Springs, a planned village centered around an award-winning golf course. For a daily fee, families staying at Woodloch Springs can participate in any activities at Woodloch Pines.

Woodloch Pines and Woodloch Springs are four-season resorts, with plenty to do and see no matter what the weather outside. Rates for the all-inclusive family resort at Woodloch Pines start at $140 to $180 per adult for a two-night stay during Thanksgiving week (the first child under twelve in the same room stays free; charge for additional children varies according to age) and rise to $1050 per adult for a week-long, mid-summer stay in the best accommodations available.

At Woodloch Springs, a family of four can rent a two-bedroom home for $140 a night or $800 per week from mid-October through April. During the peak summer season, a two-bedroom home is available for $240 per night or $1,400 per week. Three-bedroom homes are also available. American plan (all meals included) is available at an additional cost. For more information and reservations, call (800) 572–6658.

LACKAWAXEN

Route 590 continues east from Woodloch Pines to the state line at Lackawaxen and the Delaware River. This tiny Pennsylvania town was the home of Zane Grey, author of such famous Western novels as *The Riders of the Purple Sage* and more than fifty others. Today the property is owned by the National Park Service as part of the **Upper Delaware Scenic and Recreational River,** which encompasses a 74-mile stretch of river from Matamoras to Winterdale.

The **Zane Grey Museum** (River Road, 717–685–4871) houses an impressive collection of memorabilia of Grey's life and his passion for the West. Little ones will be frustrated by the "don't touch" policy of the museum, but school-aged and older kids interested in stories of the Wild West will enjoy the twenty-minute guided tour. If you luck out and get an individual tour, the guide may be able to gear his or her presentation to your family's interests. Admission is free. Call ahead for museum hours.

Also at the museum is a gift shop (many of Grey's novels are on sale for some light vacation reading). The ranger on duty will be able to point out some of the highlights of the park, including the locks of the **D&H Canal.** Be sure to ask for the Junior Ranger Program Activity Book. Children who successfully complete six of the twelve activities in the pamphlet are awarded with a certificate of achievement and a Junior Ranger patch.

After checking out the museum, take a stroll down to the river and across the **Roebling Bridge,** the oldest wire suspension bridge in the country. It was designed and built in 1848 by John Augustus Roebling—the man who later designed the famous Brooklyn Bridge in New York City.

There's also a river access in Lackawaxen for fishing boats and rafting. If you don't have your own boat to launch here, contact one of the liveries that rent canoes, rafts, and tubes and conduct guided trips down the Delaware. The Park Service publishes a list of liveries and licensed guides. Some of the bigger operations on the river include: Kittatinny Canoes (800–356–2852); Lander's River Trips (800–252–2925); and Wild and Scenic River Tours (800–836–0366). All of these outfitters provide boats, life jackets, and drop-off and pick-up service at various river access points. They also have campsites available, although most are located on the New York side of the river.

Both the Delaware and the Lackawaxen rivers are known as prime fly-fishing areas. Licensed guides will take you and your older kids out on the river for lessons. Try the **Delaware River Fly Fishing School and Guide Service** (717–798–2753) or check the list published by the park service.

For more information about touring the Upper Delaware River Valley, contact the National Park Service (717–685–4871 or 729–8251) or the Upper Delaware Council, an organization of businesses and individuals along the

New York and Pennsylvania shores of the river (914–252–3022).

BEACH LAKE

Beach Lake, located on Route 652, makes a great home base for exploring the Upper Delaware.

Central House, with its on-the-lake location, family-style meals, and on-site swimming pool and volleyball court, is a nice spot for a value-priced family vacation. Room rates start at around $35 per night in the off-season, $50 in summer. Call (717) 729–7411 or 729–8341.

For families who prefer to cook their own meals, the **Pine Grove Cabins** can't be beat. Owners Jerry and Barbara Zimmerman keep this bungalow colony immaculate. The cabins are tiny, but there's a kitchen, small living room, a bathroom with shower, and two bedrooms crammed into each one. The property is right on the lake, with a sandy beach for swimming and rowboats for guest use. Guests bring their own sheets and do their own cooking, but the rates are reasonable: $55 per night per cabin, with special week-long packages available. For more information, call (717) 729–8522.

Across Route 652, **Carousel Water & Fun Park** is great for kids of all ages. Go-karts, water slides, bumper boats, mini-golf, and batting cages are among the attractions here. Pay one price or pay by the ride. For more information, call (717) 729–7532.

HONESDALE

Honesdale, located at the intersection of routes 6 and 191, is in many ways the quintessential American small town. Its Main Street is lined with shops and stores that have been operated by the same families for years. Through a special Main Street program, many of the stores have been renovated to reflect the town's historic architecture. And the Victorian homes and big porches of north Main Street are classic examples of American design.

The center for all this historic activity is the **Wayne County Historical Society,** located in two historic buildings at 810 Main Street. Here you can see a replica of the original *Stourbridge Lion,* the first steam locomotive to run on an American rail in 1829. (The original is in the Smithsonian Institution in Washington, D.C.) Other exhibits trace the history of the D&H Canal (which connected Honesdale to the Hudson River, 108 miles away) and the coal industry. There's also an impressive collection of Native American artifacts found in the Delaware Valley by a local collector.

The museum is open Monday through Saturday 10:00 A.M. to 4:00 P.M.

during June through September. Call (717) 253–3240 for off-season hours or more information. Admission is $2.00 for adults; $1.00 for children twelve to eighteen. Children under twelve are admitted free.

At the Wayne County Chamber of Commerce at 742 Main Street, you can purchase tickets for the **Stourbridge Rail Excursions,** which run on weekends in summer and for special occasions at other times. The excursions follow the Lackawaxen River to Hawley and Lackawaxen. Different themes include fall foliage tours, dinner theater tours, the Great Train Robbery Run, the Halloween Fun Run, and the Santa Express. Rates vary according to season and itinerary. For more information, call the Chamber of Commerce at (717) 253–1960.

After your rail excursion or walking tour, treat yourself and the kids to scrumptious desserts and coffees at the **Main Street Beanery** (1139 Main Street; 717–253–5740). Set up like an old-time ice cream parlor, this restaurant serves up ice cream sundaes, milk shakes, and egg creams with great names like the Big Green Ugly. What kid could resist? During the summer, there's a garden out back for outdoor eating.

STARLIGHT

Head north from Honesdale on Route 191 and you'll find yourself in northern Wayne County. The thick forests of this corner of the state add to the feeling of an escape from civilization.

One of the best places to enjoy northern Wayne County is the **Inn at Starlight Lake,** which has been attracting vacationers since 1909. Guests can stay in the inn itself, but families will generally prefer the cottages. Each cottage is a little different: Some have fireplaces, others have sleeping lofts for kids. All have private bathrooms.

The inn, as the name suggests, is located right on Starlight Lake, a pretty little body of water that's great for swimming and exploring by rowboat or small sailboat (no powerboats allowed). There are tennis courts, shuffleboard, and a library and a game room for evenings and rainy days. In winter, the inn maintains miles of groomed trails for cross-country skiing. Bring your own equipment or rent from the inn.

The inn is also the first stop on a five-day self-guided inn-to-inn bike tour of Wayne and Susquehanna counties. For families with older children, this is a great combination of an active vacation and lovely accommodations.

Summer rates at the Inn at Starlight Lake start at $126 per night for two people, including breakfast and dinner. Children under seven are free (food is charged à la carte). Weekly rates are also available. Rates are generally lower in winter. For more information, call (717) 798–2519 or (800) 248–2519.

NEW MILFORD

To reach New Milford, head west from Starlight, following small country roads toward Route 81. Just a few miles from the interstate (follow the signs) is **Old Mille Village Museum,** a group of historic buildings and artifacts depicting life in the area in the 1800s. Each weekend, during the summer, artisans demonstrate different crafts, from blacksmithing to quilting. There are also special events and festivals throughout the season, including Annual Arts and Crafts Day, an antique doll show, Old Time Country Music Contest, and more.

Hours and days of operation vary from year to year. Admission is $4.00 for adults, $1.00 for children nine to twelve. Children under nine are admitted free. Call (717) 465–3448 for more information.

SCRANTON

Until the recent grand opening of the **Steamtown National Historic Site** in downtown Scranton, this industrial city was hardly thought of as a vacation destination. However, those attracted by one of the nation's newest national parks are often pleasantly surprised that Scranton has a lot to offer—especially to family travelers.

Railroad buffs won't want to miss Steamtown. Occupying forty acres of a working railroad yard in downtown Scranton, Steamtown traces the history of railroading in the region and throughout the country. The new structure, opened in 1995, includes a visitor center, theater, technology and history museums, renovated roundhouse, and bookstore.

Watch the twenty-minute film, *Steel and Steam,* to learn about the history of American steam railroading. At the history museum, meet the people (actually life-like statues) who worked, used, and depended on the railroad. Visit the roundhouse to see several examples from the Steamtown collection of more than one hundred railroad cars. Learn about locomotive design and railroad communications at the technology museum. And don't miss the scale model of the Scranton yard as it appeared in 1937.

From Steamtown, you can arrange to take a train excursion to the nearby town of Moscow or the **Historic Scranton Iron Furnaces** (717–963–3208), just a short hop away. Occasionally, the park plans longer excursions, such as a day-trip to Binghamton, New York, or an overnight visit to Syracuse. Call the park for more information and schedules. The visitor center and most of the railroad yard and outdoor exhibits are free. Entry to the museums and the theater is $6.00 for adults, $2.00 for children five to fifteen years old. If you plan to take a train ride to Moscow, you'll save money with a combination ticket. For more information, contact (717) 340–5200.

FAITH AND EMILY'S FAVORITE EVENTS IN NORTHEASTERN PENNSYLVANIA

Ice Tee Golf Tournament (mid-February) Lake Wallenpaupack (717) 226–3191
Patch Town Day (mid-June) Eckley Miners' Village (717) 636–2070
Troy Fair (late July) Troy (717) 297–3405
Moscow Country Fair (mid-August) Moscow (717) 842–9804
Shawnee Mountain Lumberjack Festival (early October) Shawnee-on-Delaware (717) 421–7231

After touring Steamtown, walk up the long ramp to the **Steamtown Mall.** There's a food court with fast food for every taste. If you prefer a more leisurely dining experience, head downstairs, where there are two restaurants to choose from.

Sticking with the railroad motif, why not stay in a glorious old railway station? The **Lackawanna Station Hotel,** a National Register building now operated by the Radisson chain of hotels, is located at 700 Lackawanna Avenue, just a few blocks from Steamtown. The station's waiting area has been transformed into a palatial lobby with two restaurants and complete hotel facilities. Room rates start at $89 a night. Suites, some with kitchenette, go for $179 per night. Children under eighteen stay for free. For reservations or more information, call (717) 342–8300.

Who can resist a magician? The **Houdini Museum** at 1433 North Main Avenue in Scranton is a must-see for budding magicians. The museum takes visitors back to the days of vaudeville, when traveling performers like Houdini frequently visited the Scranton area. There are daily magic shows from Memorial Day to Labor Day, along with Houdini memorabilia and exhibits about Scranton's vaudeville past. Admission is $7.50 for adults, $6.00 for children. Open in summer, 10:00 A.M. to 6:00 P.M. daily. For more information call (717) 342–5555 or 342–8527.

Coal is a major part of this region's history. One of the best places to gain an understanding of the life of a coal miner is on the **Lackawanna Coal Mine Tour** at McDade Park in Scranton. Here visitors ride 300 feet down into a real underground coal mine. Former miners and sons of miners tell the story of what a typical work day was like for the men and boys (as young as seven years old!) of the mines. It's chilly and damp down below, so be sure to bring along a sweatshirt. Admission is $7.00 for adults; $5.00 for children. Call (717) 963–MINE for more information.

Next door, also in McDade Park, is the **Anthracite Heritage Museum,** which traces the history of coal and its influence on the people of this area, from the Paleo Indians to immigrant workers in the coal mines. Call (717) 963–4804 for more information.

McDade Park is also home to a summer theater festival, a fall balloon festival, and other special events. In addition it's a great place for a family picnic and outdoor play. For more information and a schedule of upcoming events, call (717) 963–6764.

Another center of family-oriented activity is **Montage Mountain,** located on the opposite side of Scranton. During the winter months, Montage is a ski resort with a 1,000-foot vertical drop and twenty slopes to choose from. In the off-season, Montage becomes a performing arts center and family fun spot with special concerts, water slides, batting cages, chair lift rides, children's activity park, playground, and more. The summer park is open from mid-June to Labor Day, weekdays noon to 5:00 P.M.; weekends, 11:00 A.M. to 5:00 P.M. Admission to the water slides and aqua slide is $6.95 per individual, $19.95 for a family of four or more. For more information about the ski resort, concert schedule, family park, or other special events, call (717) 969–7669 or (800) GOT–SNOW. Nearby, the **Lackawanna County Stadium** is home to the Red Barons, a AAA farm club for the Philadelphia Phillies. For game information and schedules for the upcoming season, call (717) 969–BALL.

In Nay Aug Park, check out what's at the **Everhart Museum.** Their permanent exhibits include a dinosaur hall, fossil display, and bird gallery as well as examples of American and European painting, prints, and more. The Everhart often attracts high-quality traveling exhibits (such as Dinamation's Dinosaurs Alive!), so be sure to call ahead (717–346–8370) and see what will be there during your stay.

If your family enjoys air shows, schedule a visit to the Scranton area for mid-August, to coincide with the **Annual Armed Forces Air Show,** billed as the premier air show in the Northeast. It's held at the Wilkes-Barre/Scranton International Airport in Acoca, located on Route 81 between Scranton and Wilkes-Barre. Precision formation flying, parachuters, aerial ballet, tactical demonstrations, and other in-the-air performances complement a full array of land-based exhibits of aircraft. Admission is $8.00 for adults, $4.00 for children six to twelve. For more information about the upcoming air show and other special events and vacation opportunities in the Scranton area, call the Northeast Territory Visitor's Bureau at (800) 22–WELCOME.

FREELAND

Just 9 miles east of Route 81 near Freeland, **Eckley Miners' Village** offers the chance to visit an authentic nineteenth-century "patch" town. The town was originally built in 1854 by the mining firm of Sharpe, Leisenring and Co. for its workers, mostly new immigrants to the States. The town, which was restored in the late 1960s for the filming of the movie *The Molly Maguires*, is now an historic site, administered by the Pennsylvania Historical and Museum Commission. Throughout the summer season, the village holds various special events, including Patch Town Day, a Civil War Encampment, and Family Sunday, which features a community picnic typical of the 1800s.

Eckley Miners' Village is open Monday through Saturday 9:00 A.M. to 5:00 P.M. and Sundays noon to 5:00 P.M. Admission is $3.50 for adults, $2.50 for seniors, and $1.50 for children six to seventeen. Guided tours are available in summer months for an additional $1.00 per person. For more information, call (717) 636–2070.

JIM THORPE

In the late 1800s and early 1900s, tourists flocked to Mauch Chunk (now Jim Thorpe) to ride the famous **Switchback Railroad.** This 18-mile figure-8 of track was more like a roller-coaster than a train ride—at some points on the trip, cars reached speeds of 60 miles per hour. Now, in the late 1900s, the Switchback is again attracting tourists. Although the railroad has not operated in many years, its railbed has been transformed into one of the best-known mountain bike trails on the East Coast.

The Switchback Trail is just one reason to visit the lovely town of Jim Thorpe. For a family that wants to combine outdoor activities like biking, hiking and swimming with more urbane pursuits such as museums, shops, and restaurants, Jim Thorpe has a winner combination.

In town, stroll the streets of the **Historic Victorian Village.** At the Visitor's Center in the old Jersey Central Railroad Station, pick up brochures about local activities and attractions. This is also the starting point for a number of special train ride excursions. For schedule and fare information, contact Rail Tours, Inc. at (717) 325–4606.

Across the parking lot, in the Hooven Mercantile Co. building, head up to the second floor to see the **Scale Model Railroad Display.** With 1,000 feet of track, 60 cars, 200 miniature buildings, and 100 bridges, it sure is an impressive display. Opening hours vary. Call (717) 325–2248 for more information. Continue on up Broadway and get a feel for the town some call "Little Switzerland." Stop in at the **Mauch Chunk Museum and Cultural Center** (41 West Broadway) to learn about the history of the Switchback Railroad and the town that grew up around it. There's also a display about the life of Jim Thorpe, the Native American Olympic althlete for whom the town was renamed in the 1950s. Although Thorpe was never a resident of the town, his widow heard of the area's efforts to revitalize its economy and offered her husband's memorabilia in exchange for naming the town in his honor.

Head up the street to the **Old Jail Museum.** This building served as the Carbon County jail from 1871 to January 1995. Purchased by Thomas and Betty Lou McBride, it has now been preserved as a museum. Tour guides take visitors through the kitchen, cell blocks, even down to the basement where prisoners were kept in solitary confinement. It's a bit spooky, but there are lessons to be learned here. Older kids especially seem fascinated. The Old Jail Museum is open daily from Memorial Day to October 31, noon to 4:00 P.M. Admission is $4.00 for adults, $3.50 for students with I.D., and $2.50 for children six to twelve.

If mountain biking or other outdoor sports are your pleasure, stop in at the **Blue Mountain Bike Shop** (34 Susquehanna Street, 717–325–4421) for information about the excellent trails in the area. The store offers top-quality bike rentals and shuttle service to various trail heads. Tell the experienced staff your skill level and how much time you want to spend, and they'll guide you to the right trail. Bike rentals run from $5.00 to $8.00 per hour or $20 to $40 per day, including helmet, water bottle, and map. Shuttle service is $10.00 per person, $15.00 if you have your own equipment. In addition to bike rentals, the store has camping equipment, kayaks, rowboats, canoes, cross-country skis, and snowshoes for rent.

Much of the Switchback trail is located within or near **Mauch Chunk Lake Park,** a county park that offers more than a vacation's worth of activities. The park features nice campsites, a sandy beach on a beautiful lake, excellent programs at the environmental center and 18 miles of biking, hiking, or cross-country skiing trails. On weekends during the month of October— peak foliage time—the park offers hayrides along the Switchback Trail. Fees for the rides are $2.50 for adults, $1.25 for children. For more information about hayrides, camping, and other park facilities, call (717) 325–3669.

Another option for outdoor enthusiasts is a rafting trip down the Lehigh River. **Pocono Whitewater Adventures** offers "Family-Style Floatrips" for kids from "five to eighty-five." Rates for a summer floatrip start at $19 for children up to sixteen years old and $32 for adults. Call (717) 325–8430 for information.

Gather the gang and hit the road on two wheels for a beautiful ride along the Lehigh River.
(Courtesy Martin Livezey)

LEHIGHTON

If you enjoyed the model train display in Jim Thorpe, then head south to see the even larger display at the **Pocono Museum Unlimited,** located on Route 443 just west of Lehighton. The display measures 117 feet by 32 feet and features sixteen operating trains and 2006 feet of track in a complete miniature environment, with waterfalls, drive-in movie theater, zoo, amusement park, 40-foot lake, and more. Admission is $4.00 for adults, $2.00 for children ages five to twelve. Call (717) 386–3117 for more information.

ANDREAS

To continue a transportation tour, from trains to cars, travel on Route 443 west to Andreas, and the **JEM Classic Car Museum,** an 18,000-square-foot display floor that features an impressive collection of antique automobiles. The collection belongs to John E. Morgan, who began buying vintage cars more than thirty years ago. Recently, Morgan has branched out to large-scale model airplanes and a display of American and foreign dolls.

The museum is open from May 30 to October 31 weekdays 10:00 A.M. to 4:00 P.M. and weekends noon to 4:00 P.M. Admission is $4.00 for adults, $2.50 for children five to twelve. Call (717) 386–3554 for more information.

ASHLAND

If you didn't visit the Lackawanna Coal Mine in Scranton—or if you and your kids enjoyed it so much you're ready for another mine tour—then head to Ashland and the **Pioneer Tunnel Coal Mine.** Like the Scranton mine, this is an actual coal mine. When the coal company shut it down, some local volunteers and former miners transformed it into a fascinating study of a coal miner's life. Visitors enter the mine in open mine cars, just like the miners did when they started their workdays.

After the thirty-five-minute mine tour, take a ride on a narrow-gauge steam locomotive, the *Henry Clay.* Along the 1.5-mile round-trip, you'll see two other examples of coal mining: a strip mine and a bootleg coal mine, where men snuck past guards to get coal to sell or to heat their own homes.

The mine and steam tour are open 10:00 A.M. to 6:00 P.M. daily from Memorial Day to Labor Day, weekends during May, September, and October. Admission is charged. Call (717) 875–3850 for more information.

While in Ashland, stop at the **Museum of Anthracite Mining,** located at 17th and Pine streets in the town of Ashland. Call (717) 636–2070 for more information.

RICKETTS GLEN STATE PARK

Ricketts Glen State Park may well be the most beautiful and least well-known of Pennsylvania's many state parks. The park, which spills into Luzerne, Sullivan, and Columbia counties, covers 13,050 acres with lakes, waterfalls (twenty-two in all!), hiking and cross-country skiing trails, and many opportunities for fishing, boating, camping, horseback-riding, and more.

The Glens Natural Area, a registered National Natural Landmark, is the centerpiece of the park. Here, where two branches of Kitchen Creek create deep gorges, there are rare stands of virgin hemlock and other trees, some more than 500 years old. Much of the hiking in the park covers pretty steep territory, but with the help of a park ranger, you can choose trails that may be easier for children. For example, the Evergreen Trail, just half a mile long, takes hikers through giant hemlocks and pine trees and to a view of several waterfalls. There are 120 tent and trailer campsites available year-round at the park. In summer there are flush toilets and hot showers. In winter, only pit toilets are available.

If camping sounds a bit too rustic, consider staying at one of the ten comfortable family cabins in the park. Each has a living area, kitchen, bath, and two or three bedrooms. Advance reservations are required for the cabins.

Hunting is permitted in parts of the park. If you visit during the hunting season (primarily in late fall), check in with park rangers to find out what safety precautions are appropriate. For more information, call the park directly at (717) 477–5675 or for general State Park information, call (800) 63PARKS.

FORKSVILLE

Forksville might as well be called Festiville, with all the annual events planned for the fairgrounds and other locations around town. The fun starts in January with the annual **Endless Mountains 50 Sled Dog Race.** The 50-mile race, which is run in the state game lands near Forksville, attracts six-dog racing teams from as far away as Canada and Alaska.

In February, the Forksville fairgrounds is the site of the **Forksville Sleigh Ride and Rally.** Here, horses pull the sleighs. In addition to divisions for men, women, and children, there's a timed obstacle course race and a "Currier & Ives" class, where contestants are judged on the "postcard" quality of their sleighs. July brings the **Sullivan Country Rodeo and Truck Pull** and at the end of summer, the **Sullivan County Fair** is held at the Forksville Fairgrounds. In October, it's time for the **Flaming Foliage Festival,** with demonstrations by quilters, woodcarvers, and apple butter and apple cider makers. There are wagon rides, draft horses, and lots of activities for children.

For more information and a schedule of upcoming events in Forksville, contact the Sullivan County Chamber of Commerce at (717) 946–4160 or the Endless Mountains Visitors Bureau at (717) 836–5431.

Another attraction in Forksville is **World's End State Park.** Despite its small size (less than 1,000 acres), it's easy to feel like you're at the edge of the world in this remote valley. If you're looking for a good place to introduce your children to wilderness camping, this is the spot. There are seventy tent and trailer camp sites and nineteen cabins, equipped with refrigerator, range, fireplace, table, chairs, and beds. (There's a central shower facility.)

The park includes numerous hiking trails including the Loyalsock Trail, a 59$\frac{3}{10}$-mile hike, part of which runs through the park. Most of the trails are pretty steep, so this park is a better choice for older kids and more experienced hikers. For more information, call the park directly at (717) 924–3287 or call (800) 63PARKS for general state park information.

TROY

Young and old alike will enjoy the **Farm Museum** recently established by the Bradford County Heritage Association near the Troy Fairgrounds. A re-created barn holds local resident and dairy farmer Wilmer Wilcox's impressive collection of farm antiques. The displays work together to tell the story of rural farm life in Bradford County. There's a bedroom area, a kitchen, and antique cloth-ing. You'll also see a craftsmen's area with rotating displays and demonstrations of blacksmithing, carpentry, and tinsmithing, as well as a doctor's office and an old country store.

The museum is open 10:00 A.M. to 4:00 P.M. Friday to Sunday and holidays from the end of April to the end of October. Admission is $2.50 for adults, $1.00 for children. Children under the age of six are free. The museum is open daily during the **Troy Fair,** a typical country fair with farm animals, agricultural displays, and amusements, which has usually been held each year for the last 120, toward the end of July. For more information about the museum, call (717) 297–3410. For more about the Troy Fair, call (717) 297–3648.

NORTHWESTERN AND CENTRAL PENNSYLVANIA

According to 1990 U.S. Census data, Pennsylvania has the largest rural population in the country. That means there are more people living in towns of fewer than 2,500 people here than in any other state in the country. Although all of the regions covered in this book have many towns that meet that description, in Northwestern and Central Pennsylvania, it's hard to find towns that don't. In fact, there are large stretches of this region that remain wilderness—and provide wonderful opportunities for camping, boating, hiking, skiing, and more.

Of course, there's more to this area than just trees and mountains. State College is home to Penn State University, one of the finest public universities in the country. In fact, the center of the state holds a wonderful array of cultural, historical, and recreational opportunities for families. There's so much packed into that area that we decided to give it its own section of this chapter.

The rest of the region is a mecca for nature lovers. Pine Creek Gorge is billed as Pennsylvania's Grand Canyon and is a spectacular achievement of nature. Allegheny National Forest is one of only fifteen national forests in the eastern United States and harbors some of the last remaining virgin stands of northern hardwoods left in the East.

This is a big area. Our advice would be to keep your ambitions within

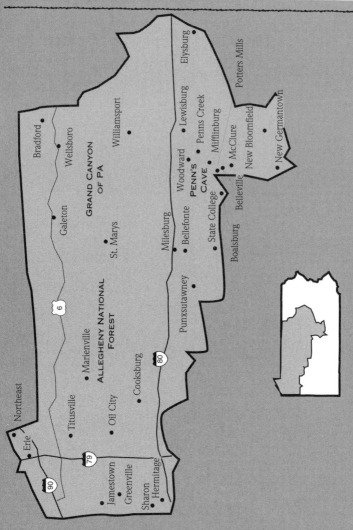

Elysburg

Potters Mills

Lewisburg

Penns Creek

Mifflinburg

New Germantown

Bradford

Wellsboro

Williamsport

GRAND CANYON OF PA

Woodward

PENN'S CAVE

McClure

New Bloomfield

Galeton

Milesburg

Bellefonte

Belleville

St. Marys

State College

Boalsburg

ALLEGHENY NATIONAL FOREST

Marienville

Punxsutawney

6

Cooksburg

80

Northeast

Titusville

Oil City

Erie

79

Jamestown

Greenville

Sharon

Hermitage

90

Northwestern and Central
Pennsylvania

limits. Pick a state park, a town, or a sight that interests you most, and build your vacation around it. Try to see more than a portion of this region, and you'll spend more time in the car than enjoying its many offerings. You can always come back to see more at another time.

ELYSBURG

If you've ever wondered what happened to the traditional amusement parks you remember from your own childhood, head to **Knoebels Amusement Park and Campground,** located on Route 487, about 12 miles south of Bloomsburg. This park got its start at the turn of the century when Henry Hartman Knoebel (pronounced with a hard "k") charged 25 cents to water, feed, and brush the horses that brought groups to swim on his property. After a few years, he added picnic tables and sold ice cream and other snacks to the visitors. A pool, overnight cottages, and a carousel were added in 1926. By the 1940s, Knoebels had graduated to an amusement resort.

Today, Knoebels offers forty rides (including four giant water slides), a giant swimming pool, several restaurants and snack bars, picnic areas, 500 campsites, log cabins, and tepees for overnight accommodations, and a collection of shops and regular entertainment. All of this is nestled among natural streams and shady hemlock trees that keep the temperatures here a good ten degrees lower than elsewhere in the area.

Knoebels is a great place for a day trip or, for real amusement park fans, a two- or three-day stay. Open weekends in April, May, and September; daily June, July, and August. Admission to the park is free. Rides are "moderately priced." Camping starts at $18 a night, $115 per week. Cabins sleep six, have electricity, and cost $55 a night. Tepee rental is $39 per night. Call (717) 672–2572 for park information; (717) 672–9555 for campground information.

PENNS CREEK

On Route 104, just south of the town of Penns Creek, **Walnut Acres Organic Farms** has been growing fruits, grains, and vegetables without pesticides for nearly fifty years. The farm is also home to a thriving mail-order business and a farm store. Visitors are welcome to take a self-guided tour of the property. Most of the trails are 1 mile or less, suitable to little legs or even strollers. On weekdays, tours are given of the plant, where fresh fruits and vegetables are canned and packaged. The farm store is open 9:00 A.M. to 5:00 P.M. Monday through Saturday and from noon to 5:00 P.M. on Sunday. Lunch is served in the store 11:00 A.M. to 2:00 P.M. Monday through Saturday. Call (800) 433–3998.

LEWISBURG

A pretty Victorian town that is home to Bucknell University, Lewisburg is a good place to stop and stretch the legs. Pick up a walking tour brochure from the **Union County Tourist Agency** at 418 Market Street (717–524–2815). There are several houses open for tours, including the **Packwood House Museum** (15 North Water Street) and the **Slifer House Museum** (1 River Road). Neither is especially appropriate for small children, however. There is an impressive collection of children's furniture and toys at the Packwood, but they're only a small part of the tour.

Train lovers will want to climb aboard one of the rail excursions departing from **Delta Place Station,** located on Route 15 in Lewisburg. Two different routes are offered: a one-and-a-half-hour round-trip through Lewisburg, along the Susquehanna River and the Buffalo Mountains to the nearby town of Winfield, and a two-and-a-half-hour round-trip through the Amish and Mennonite farmland of the Buffalo Valley to the town of Mifflinburg (see below). The latter trip is only available on Sundays from June through October. Delta Place Station also offers dinner trains and special theme rides, including a Great Train Robbery one day a week, a Haunted Train Ride at the end of October, and the Santa Claus Express in December. For more information and current rates and schedules, call (717) 524–4337.

MIFFLINBURG

If you've been admiring the buggies that the Amish and some Mennonite families use to get around, why not stop at the **Mifflinburg Buggy Museum** at 523 Green Street. At the turn of the century, Mifflinburg was a center of buggymaking, with as many as fifty different buggy works in operation at one time. The museum consists of the home and factory of William A. Heiss, owner of William A Heiss Coach Works. The shop was rescued from abandonment by community volunteers around the time of the country's Bicentennial and it is now on the National Register of Historic Places.

Visitors can tour the house and the factory, both of which have been restored to the way they would have looked when the company was in full swing. Upstairs in the shop is a display of sleighs. The museum is open Thursday through Sunday 1:00 to 5:00 P.M. May through mid-September. Over Memorial Day weekend, the museum is the headquarters for **Mifflinburg Buggy Days,** a street festival that the whole town participates in with buggy rides, locally made foods, games, and more.

Another Mifflinburg traditional celebration is **Christkindl Market,** held the Thursday through Sunday after Thanksgiving each year. The festival re-creates a traditional German Christmas, with authentic food, seasonal music, and handmade gifts for sale. For more information call (717) 966–1666.

WILLIAMSPORT

If you've got a child in Little League, then Williamsport is a required stop on your vacation in Central Pennsylvania. The **Peter J. McGovern Little League Baseball Museum** traces the history of Little League from its founding in 1939 to today, when more than two and a half million children in eighty countries participate in the program. There are interactive displays and batting cages with instant replay monitors so kids can see themselves at bat. You can watch highlights of the Little League World Series—a truly international sporting event that takes place here each August. The Hall of Excellence includes tributes to such famous former Little Leaguers as Tom Seaver, Kareem Abdul-Jabbar, columnist George Will, and New Jersey Senator Bill Bradley.

The museum is open every day except Thanksgiving, Christmas, and New Year's Day. Hours are 9:00 A.M. to 5:00 P.M. Monday through Saturday and noon to 5:00 P.M. on Sunday. From Memorial Day to Labor Day, the museum is open until 7:00 P.M. daily. Admission is $5.00 for adults, $1.50 for children five to thirteen. A family admission (parents and all dependent children) is $13.

The museum is a great destination, but there's more to Williamsport than baseball. The **Children's Discovery Workshop** at 343 West Fourth Street is a hands-on museum for children ages three to eleven. The interactive exhibits are designed to inspire children's imaginations, explorations, and discoveries. There are clothes for dress up, bricks from which to build a castle, and more. The museum is open every day except Monday. Admission is $3.50 per person. Call ahead for hours (717–322–KIDS).

Model train enthusiasts will want to stop at the **Lycoming County Historical Society Museum,** at 400 Market Street. There's a frontier room, which re-creates the furnishings from the county's first European settlement in 1769; a general store from the turn of the century; and farming, blacksmithing, and milling tools from the 1700s to 1900s. Last but certainly not least, there's an exhibit of over 300 Shempp model trains, one of the finest collections in the country.

The museum is open Tuesday through Saturday year-round and Sundays during the summer. Admission is $3.50 for adults, $1.50 for children.

There are two great ways to tour the sights of Williamsport. One is the **Herdic Trolley,** a ninety-minute narrated trip in a replica of an old trolley. The route takes you past Millionaire's Row (6 blocks of magnificent mansions), the field where the first Little League game was played, and other sights of the city. The tours take place three days a week during the summer months. For current schedule and fare information call (717) 326–2500.

The other way to tour the town is aboard the *Hiawatha,* a paddle-wheeler that plies the Susquehanna River. The hour-long cruise includes a narration that relates the history of the area, from the time when the Susquehannock Indians lived along these shores through the European settlements and boom years of the lumber industry.

The boat leaves from Susquehanna Park on Route 220 several times a day during the summer months, Tuesday through Sunday. Weekend cruises are available during May and October. Special events include a Beach Party, Sunset Concert Cruises, Murder on the High Seas, and a Family Night, once a week. Rates are $7.00 for adults; $5.00 for children. (Special rates available on Family Nights.) Call (800) 358–9900 for current schedules and more information.

On Route 15 south of Williamsport, don't miss **Clyde Peeling's Reptiland,** an accredited zoo with a collection of fifty different species of reptiles. Vipers, boas, water moccasins, alligators (including one more than 11 feet long and 800 pounds!), giant tortoises, turtles, iguanas—they're all here. There are educational programs several times during the day that give children a chance to see and touch the animals up close. The zoo is open daily 9:00 A.M. to 7:00 P.M. May through September. October to April, the hours are 10:00 A.M. to 5:00 P.M. For more information, call (717) 538–1869.

McCLURE

If your family wants to experience farm life first-hand, then a vacation at Ken and Sally Hassinger's **Mountain Dale Farm** in McClure is just the ticket. This 175-acre farm is surrounded by state forest and game land, making it a complete get away from civilization. But you don't have to rough it completely. The farm offers accommodations in a variety of cabins and efficiencies. There is a 200-year-old restored log house that has four bedrooms and sleeps up to fourteen people (yours for a family of four for less than $99 a night!). Efficiency cabins start at $70 a night for four people and the more rustic and secluded forest cabins go for just $43 a night for four people. Children under twelve are half-price and those under two years old stay free. Meals are provided at an extra cost upon request, but most visitors enjoy cooking in their own kitchens or in the common kitchen.

Activities include boating, fishing, swimming, or ice-skating on three ponds; cross-country skiing or hiking in the woods; helping with the farm chores; or just relaxing on the front porch of your cabin. Come at Christmas time and choose your own tree from the Christmas tree farm. For more information or reservations, call (717) 658–3536.

Young visitors at the Mountain Dale Farm have fun helping with farm chores, such as hauling grain used to feed livestock. (Courtesy Mountain Dale Farm)

NEW BLOOMFIELD

In Perry County, 830-acre **Little Buffalo State Park** has both historic and natural attractions. There's an eighty-eight-acre lake, swimming pool, hiking trails, fishing, and picnic areas. But there are also a covered bridge, a working grist mill from the 1800s, and old tavern, all of which have been restored (or are in the process). In the winter, there are 7 miles of cross-country trails, a sledding and tobogganing area, and a skating area on the lake (the rest of the lake is open for ice-fishing in winter). There is no camping in the park, but the park ranger can furnish names of other campgrounds in the area. For more information, call the park at (717) 567-9255.

Just a few miles south of Little Buffalo State Park on Route 34 is the **Box Huckleberry Natural Area,** a special reserve for a box huckleberry plant estimated to be 1,300 years old. There is a short interpretive nature trail around the area. This is a good place to teach your kids about the importance of preserving our natural resources. Trail maps and a written history of the plant are available on site. For more information, call (717) 536-3191.

NEW GERMANTOWN

Traveling southwest on Route 274 from New Germantown, you'll come upon the entrance to the **Tuscarora State Forest**—90,512 acres of amazing vistas, undisturbed areas, trout streams, state parks, hiking, snowmobiling, and more. The forest roads are well-maintained, making a great route for a mild "off-road" driving experience. The Bureau of Forestry has developed a brochure that will guide you on a 26-mile auto tour of the forest. The dirt roads are in good shape, so you shouldn't need four-wheel drive to navigate the route in good weather.

Highlights in and around the state forest include: **Hemlocks Natural Area,** a 131-acre area of virgin hemlock forest with 3 miles of hiking trails; the **Iron Horse Trail,** a rails-to-trails project that provides 10 miles of hiking with only moderate climbing necessary; the **Tuscarora Trail,** a 22-mile side trail of the Appalachian Trail; **Fowler Hollow State Forest,** with eighteen campsites and fishing in the creek; and **Colonel Denning State Park,** with fifty-two trailer and tent sites, excellent hiking, and an extensive environmental education program during summer months. For more information about the State Forest and natural areas, contact the Bureau of Forestry, RD 1 Box 42-A, Blain 17006 or call (717) 536–3191. For more information about state parks, call (717) 776–5272 or (800) 63–PARKS.

BELLEVILLE

Everyone loves a farmer's market: rows of fresh vegetables, home-baked goods, handmade crafts, and the chance to meet the people who produce them. The town of Belleville may have the ultimate farmer's market. The **Belleville Auction,** an Amish farmer's market, takes place every Wednesday from 6 in the morning to 6 at night. The ten-acre market on Route 655 has livestock yards, auction barns, and 400 flea-market stalls. It's a popular event, so be prepared to walk a ways from your car to the auction areas. For more information, call the Juniata Valley Area Chamber of Commerce at (717) 248–6713.

Also on Route 655 between Belleville and Reedsville, check out the **Mifflin County Trout Hatchery** where children can fish for trout and pay only for what they catch. The Hatchery is open Wednesday and Saturday and fishing poles and bait are provided.

STATE COLLEGE AND UNIVERSITY PARK

A visit to a college campus is a great way to inspire a child's educational dreams. The home of **Penn State University,** one of the country's best public universities, State College has much to offer families. Pick up a free visitor's guide and campus map at one of the many information booths on campus or call the Lion Country Convention and Visitors Bureau at (800) 358–5466.

FAITH AND EMILY'S FAVORITE ATTRACTIONS IN CENTRAL AND NORTHWESTERN PENNSYLVANIA

Knoebels Amusement Resort, Elysburg
Little League Baseball Museum, Williamsport
Penn's Cave and Woodward Cave
Pine Creek Gorge, Wellsboro
Knox & Kane Railroad, Marienville
Cook Forest State Park, Cooksburg

Bolstered by the university population, State College is a thriving town with many shops and restaurants. It's also the site of the **Central Pennsylvania Festival of the Arts,** a five-day celebration that takes place in July each year. The first day of the festival is traditionally Children and Youth Day, featuring the creations of local children ages eight through eighteen and a wonderful procession through town in which children wear masks and carry their works of art. Life-sized puppets also take part in the procession. Story-telling, marionette performances, concerts, and more round out this not-to-be-missed event. For more information on the festival, call (814) 237–3682.

Families interested in cave exploring should contact the **Nittany Grotto,** headquartered in State College. This group of enthusiastic amateur cave explorers encourages safe and responsible cave exploring. Its members are pleased to arrange special family trips on request. In order to take advantage of this service, families may be asked to join the group at a cost of $9.00 a year. For more information, contact Keith Wheeland at (814) 238–2057.

On campus, there are several worthwhile museums. Especially interesting to kids are the **Frost Entomological Museum** (814–863–2865), with approximately half a million insects and arthropods, and the **Earth and Mineral Sciences Museum** (814–865–6427), with a collection of crystals, gems, carvings, and fossils. Both are free and open weekdays from 9:00 A.M. to 4:30 P.M.

After checking out the museums, you might want to take a spin around the indoor ice-skating rinks at the **Greenberg Indoor Sports Complex.** Open to the public year-round, the complex offers two rinks with superior surfaces. Call (814) 865–4102 to get a schedule of public sessions.

Of course, for many people the most famous aspect of Penn State is its football team. The **Nittany Lions** play in the Big Ten College Football League and sports fans come from around the country to see a game at Beaver Stadium. Call the visitors bureau (see above) to find out how to get tickets.

Near Beaver Stadium, check out the animals at the agricultural facilities of the **College of Agricultural Sciences.** See whitetail deer, sheep, cattle, horses, pigs, and tiny blue duiker deer. There's also an exhibit of flowering plants and vegetables during the summer months. The facility is open to the public daily from 9:00 A.M. to 4:00 P.M. Call (814) 865–4433 for more information and a schedule of special events.

Penn State's **Ag Progress Days** is one of the largest agricultural shows around. It takes place in mid-August each year and features horse exhibitions, demonstrations of the latest farming technologies, displays of antique farm equipment, and special programs just for kids. The site for this weekend event is the Russell E. Larson Agricultural Research Center, 9 miles southwest of State College on Route 45. Call (814) 865–2081 for more information.

On the same site as Agricultural Research Center, the **Jerome K. Pasto Agricultural Museum** traces the history of farming in America. It's open April 15 to October 15. Call ahead for scheduling information (814–865–8301).

After visiting the Agricultural Research Center, backtrack on Route 45 to Route 26 and head south. About 3 miles down the road, you'll see the turn for **Stone Valley Recreation Area** and **Shaver's Creek Environmental Center,** both administered by Penn State. After the hubbub of the active campus, this is a great place to come and wind down. Depending on the season, you can enjoy boating (canoes, rowboats, or sailboats—all of which are available for rent), fishing (trout and bass), hayrides, hiking, ice-skating (rentals available), sledding, ice-fishing, or cross-country skiing (rentals and lessons available). Open daily 8:00 A.M. to 5:00 P.M. For more information call (814) 863–0762.

At the Environmental Center, learn about the local wildlife and how injured eagles, hawks, and owls are rehabilitated in the Raptor Center. There's a bookstore with a good selection of books for children; you'll also find other wildlife accessories there. Special gardens attract butterflies, bees, and hummingbirds. The facility is open daily, 10:00 A.M. to 5:00 P.M. For information, call (814) 863–2000 or 667–3424.

Heading east from State College on Route 322 is **Tussey Mountain Ski Resort,** a great place for family skiing. At the Cub House Learning Center, children ages three to six can enjoy two hours of play and an introduction to skiing on the "Little Bear" slopes in the Paw Prints group. The Cat Tracks group, for children six to ten years old, is aimed at building children's skiing skills. The Paw Prints session costs $10, $15 with rentals. Cat Tracks runs $15, $20 with rentals.

Lift ticket prices for adults start at just $10.00 on weekdays; $7.00 for juniors. Rentals cost extra. For more information call (814) 466–6266.

BOALSBURG

Looking for a special way to spend the upcoming three-day weekend? The tiny town of Boalsburg has several claims to fame that make it a good destination any time of year. For Memorial Day weekend, how about visiting the place where the holiday got its start? Boalsburg has been commemorating this day since 1864. Today, there are community picnics and parades to enjoy.

In July, Boalsburg is the site of the **Peoples' Choice Festival of Pennsylvania Arts and Crafts.** The weekend of activities includes free museum tours for children, a petting zoo, and a stuffed animal vet.

Columbus Day weekend coming up? What better place to get in touch with the discoverer of the New World than at the **Christopher Columbus Family Chapel,** part of the **Boal Mansion and Museum** on old Route 322 in Boalsburg. The chapel was originally part of the Columbus family castle in Spain and contains heirlooms that date back to the 1400s. The *Wall Street Journal* called the collection, "A strong tangible link to Columbus in the New World." The museum is open from May 1 to October 31 every day except Tuesday. Fall and spring hours are 1:30 to 5:00 P.M.; summer hours start at 10:00 A.M. Call (814) 466–6210.

And, for Veterans' Day, learn the history of our nation's veterans across Route 322 at the **Pennsylvania Military Museum** (814–466–6210). Starting with Ben Franklin's first military unit, the museum traces the history of the military—and Pennsylvanians' involvement—all the way through the Vietnam conflict. The museum building is surrounded by a sixty-five-acre park that includes equipment, monuments, and memorials. The museum is open Tuesday through Saturday 9:00 A.M. to 5:00 P.M. and Sunday noon to 5:00 P.M. Admission is charged.

POTTERS MILLS

Continuing east on Route 322, stop at the **Happy Valley Friendly Farm** (814–364–1904) in Potters Mills. Especially good for toddlers, this "hands-on" farm provides a safe place where children can feed and touch chicks, lambs, and other farm animals. Hayrides are available throughout the season and you can pick your own pumpkin in the fall. There's a shady picnic area, so bring your lunch and enjoy the day. The farm is open mid-April through October: Tuesday through Saturday 10:00 A.M. to 6:00 P.M., Sunday noon to 6:00 P.M. Admission is charged.

PENN'S CAVE

Kids love caves. **Penn's Cave** has been attracting visitors for centuries, since the Seneca Indians discovered it. It has been a tourist attraction since the late 1800s when a hotel was built on the site.

Penn's Cave is the country's only water-filled cave and tours are given by motorboat. Along the hour-long ride you'll see amazing stalactites and stalagmites. (Do you know the difference?) No matter what the temperature outside, it's always 52 degrees inside the cave, so bring a jacket in summertime. Tours are given daily from February 15 to December 31. Call for tour schedules and rates: (814) 364–1664.

But there's more to Penn's Cave than the cave. There's also 1,000 acres with an operating farm and a wildlife sanctuary with elk, mountain lions, deer, wolves, and mustangs. Professional guides take you through the park in four-wheel-drive vehicles, pointing out animals and telling about their habits. Tours last about one and a half hours. The sanctuary is open daily March through November. Call ahead for rates and reservations: (814) 364–1664.

In September Penn's Cave is also the site of the **Nittany Antique Machinery** annual show. Model trains, tractor parades, demonstrations of antique machinery, toy tractors, and children's pedal pull are among the attractions.

WOODWARD

If Penn's Cave has whet your appetite for spelunking, head back to Route 45 and continue east to **Woodward Cave and Campground,** one of the largest caverns in Pennsylvania. A sixty-minute tour takes you through the five rooms of the cavern, each filled with rock formations. The Hanging Forest features a large collection of stalactites. In the Hall of Statues, see one of the largest stalagmites in the United States: the Tower of Babel. The cave is open for tours daily March 15 to November 15. Call ahead for hours and admission costs. If you're planning to camp in the area, inquire about the nineteen-acre campground with sites for tents as well as RVs.

BELLEFONTE

In 1996 the historic town of Bellefonte celebrates its bicentennial. With an historic district of over 300 buildings, taking a walking tour through this town is like taking a walk back in time. Pick up a copy of "Historical Walking Tour of Bellefonte," a brochure you'll find at the train station in town. The town is especially beautiful when decked out for a Victorian Christmas each December.

When you're tired of walking, climb aboard one of the rail excursions offered by the **Bellefonte Historical Railroad.** The train station is located across the High Street Bridge. On weekends from Memorial Day to Labor Day, the railroad offers trips to Curtin Village (see below), Sayers Dam (a nice place for a picnic), the town of Lemont, or the gliderport at Julian. In the fall, the route takes you to Bald Eagle Ridge, aflame with autumn leaves. The Santa Claus Express in December features a visit from you-know-who. Other excursions are offered throughout the year. For more information and current rates and schedules, call (814) 355–0311.

MILESBURG

Heading north on Route 150 from Bellefonte, stop off at **Eagle Iron Works and Curtin Village,** an historic site that gives a glimpse of life in the 1800s. There's a restored iron furnace, the iron master's mansion and a worker's log cabin. Throughout the year, the museum holds special events, including craft shows, Civil War encampments, and antique tool demonstrations. The museum is open weekends in May, September and October and daily during the summer. It is also open in mid-December for Christmas at Curtin. Admission is $4.00 for adults; children ages six to twelve are $1.00. Call ahead for a schedule of special events (814–355–1982).

WELLSBORO

Located on scenic Route 6 in Tioga County, Wellsboro is an ideal base for adventures in **Pine Creek Gorge,** Pennsylvania's Grand Canyon. Forty-seven miles long with a maximum cliff height of 1,450 feet, this majestic canyon is surrounded by hundreds of thousands of wilderness acres to explore by boat, foot, horseback, snowmobile, cross-country skis, mountain bike, and more.

When you're planning your trip, send for the current edition of the *Outdoor Adventure Guide for Pennsylvania's Grand Canyon,* published by **Pine Creek Outfitters** (RR4, Box 130B, Wellsboro 16901; 717–724–3003). Whether you're looking for trail maps, equipment rentals, shuttles to trailheads, camping permits, guide service, you-name-it, the folks at Pine Creek Outfitters are the ones to talk to. If they can't provide it themselves, they'll point you in the right direction. For families with young children, they particularly recommend their Upper Pine half-day trip, which navigates a calm section of the creek. There is no minimum age on this trip; others have a minimum age of twelve. Once the new Rails-to-Trails bike path opens in 1996, Pine Creek will be leading guided bike tours through the Canyon as well.

There are four state parks near Pine Creek Gorge. **Leonard Harrison State Park** is on the east rim of the canyon, just south of Wellsboro. Stop at the visitors center to learn about the history of the canyon. Camping is available and there are hiking trails of varying length and difficulty. Experienced family hikers won't want to miss the "Turkey Path," a steep 1-mile journey that takes you from the rim of the canyon down to Pine Creek.

Across the canyon, **Colton Point State Park** provides a more primitive wilderness experience. There is family camping, hiking trails (during low-flow periods, you can descend this side of the canyon, cross the creek and ascend in Harrison State Park), snowmobiling, and picnic areas. For more information on both Colton and Harrison state parks, call (717) 724–3061.

Additional camping and recreation is available at **Hills Creek State Park,** east of Wellsboro (110 campsites, cabins available, one-hundred-thirty-seven-acre lake; call 717–724–4246 for more information) and **Little Pine State Park** in Waterville (103 campsites, ninety-four-acre lake, hiking and cross-country ski trails; call 717–753–8209 for more information).

Horseback riders have several options in the Wellsboro area. **Tioga Trail Rides** offers Western riding on day rides or overnight trips. Children without experience must be at least twelve years of age; children ages seven to eleven are allowed on shorter rides if they can control their horses. An hour-long ride starts at $12 per person; a day-long ride costs $63 per person, including lunch. Overnight trips start at $100 per person for groups of five to seven people. Food is included. For more information, call (717) 724–6592.

Mountain Trail Horse Center offers a wide variety of horseback adventures. During the twice-yearly Family Vacation Rides, the minimum age is dropped to eight (from the usual twelve). The two-day, one-night Family Vacation starts at $186 per person. Longer trips are available. Rates go down per person with groups over two people. Call (717) 376–5561 for more information.

For a more leisurely, less expensive, horse-drawn adventure, contact **Storms Horse Drawn Rides** outside Little Marsh, about 18 miles north of Wellsboro. Rides start at $10 per person. Call (717) 376–3481 for more information and reservations.

Wellsboro has several top-notch festivals and fairs throughout the year. Check out the **Bobsled Festival and Winter Weekend** in February, the **Pennsylvania State Laurel Festival** in June, and the **Canyon Country Blue Grass Festival** in July. For more information about festivals and other attractions in Wellsboro, contact the Chamber of Commerce at (717) 724–1926.

GALETON

From Wellsboro, head west on Route 6 to Galeton to enjoy a visit to the **Pennsylvania Lumber Museum.** Antique tools and other logging artifacts are on display. Tour a real logging camp and sawmill. The museum is the site for several unusual special events throughout the year, including the Spring Black Bear Roundup in May and the Bark Peeler's Convention in July.

The museum is open Monday through Friday in December, January, February, and March; daily in other months. Call ahead for schedule information: (814) 435–2652.

About 20 miles south of Galeton is the **Lodge at Ole Bull State Park,** voted by *Condé Nast Traveler* magazine as Pennsylvania's top getaway. The Lodge is actually a three-bedroom log cabin built by the Civilian Conservation Corps in the 1930s. It sleeps ten comfortably and is well-equipped with everything you need for a woodsy adventure. It even has a playground out back for the kids. The first floor is handicapped accessible. It rents for $335 per week, but book your reservations early. This is the kind of place where people come back each year. (Call 814–435–5000 for more information and reservations.)

Even if you're not lucky enough to book a week at the Lodge, Ole Bull is still a great place for a family adventure. There are eighty-one tent and trailer sites along Kettle Creek, some with electrical hook-ups. Swimming, hiking, fishing, biking, and cross-country skiing are all available in the secluded 125-acre park.

BRADFORD

Back on Route 6, continue west through the scenic countryside to Route 59 (at Smethport). A few miles later, head north on Route 219 toward the town of Bradford. Just before you reach Bradford, make a stop at the **Penn-Brad Oil Museum.** Just as Eastern Pennsylvania has coal, the Northwestern part of the state is oil country. This museum traces the state's involvement in oil drilling and includes a working example of the 1890s-style wooden oil rig that once dotted the country side. The museum is open daily Memorial Day through Labor Day. For more information, call (814) 362–5984.

Continuing north on Route 219, the next stop is **Crook Farm,** a collection of restored buildings from the 1800s, including a farmhouse, a one-room schoolhouse, blacksmith's shop, carpenter's shack, and barn. At the end of August, join the celebration at the **Crook Farm Country Fair** with crafts, food, entertainment, and special events for children. The museum is open Tuesday through Friday afternoons during May through September. For more information, call (814) 368–9370.

ST. MARYS

From Bradford, head south on 219 into Elk County, home of one of the two free-roaming **elk herds** east of the Mississippi—and the only one in Pennsylvania. The 1995 annual elk population survey counted 255 in the herd. One of the best places to spot the herd is near the airport in St. Marys. They also frequent the area around the town of Benezette, near Elk State Forest on Route 555. Early morning or late afternoon are the best times to see them.

Another unusual sight in St. Marys is the **Queen of the Herd** at the **Ayrshire Dairy Farm** on Old Kersey Road. Ask anyone in town how to get there; it's definitely an area landmark. Standing 15 feet tall, 20 feet long, 5 feet wide and weighing in at 1,200 pounds this fiberglass cow has stood here on the Uhl family farm for more than thirty years. The same family has owned this 500-acre dairy farm since 1919, and, if schedules allow, they'll be happy to show you around a bit.

South of St. Marys near Route 153 there's some great family programs available at **Parker Dam State Park** and **S. B. Elliot State Park.** Parker Dam offers a variety of naturalist programs for families, starting with maple sugar weekends in March all the way through apple cider Sundays in October. During the summer, there are bat programs, evening campfire talks on the weekends, and even a guided trip to see the elk herd. In summer, you can swim in the twenty-acre lake.

The camping here is Class A, which means hot showers are available. There are also rustic log frame and stone cabins available for rent year-round. There's no running water in the cabins, but there's a separate building with showers. A big fireplace supplies the heat and you can cook with an electric stove and refrigerator.

S. B. Elliot offers a quieter setting on top of a hill. There are six cabins here, but no flush toilets or showers. For more information on either park, call (814) 765–0630.

MARIENVILLE

From St. Marys, head west on Route 120 to Ridway, then catch Route 948 into **Allegheny National Forest,** the only national forest in Pennsylvania. With more than a half-million acres, there's room for many a family adventure within its boundaries.

Several towns act as good bases for explorations of the forest: Warren serves as the headquarters for the park, but there are information centers in Ridway, Custer City, Sheffield, Tionesta, and along the Allegheny Reservoir. There's also an information center in Marienville.

The forest has just about everything a family adventurer looks for: rafting, horseback-riding, camping, cabin rentals, hiking, fish hatchery, ATV and snowmobile routes, and more wildlife and wilderness than you can take in a lifetime. There are campgrounds maintained by the National Forest Service as well as privately owned ones and some in the state parks in and around the forest. For more information about visiting the Allegheny National Forest, call the headquarters at (814) 486–5150.

One way to enjoy the beauty of the forest without expending too much energy is a ride on the **Knox & Kane Railroad.** But just because you aren't hiking or biking doesn't mean you're not going to have an adventure on this 96-mile ride from Marienville to Kinzua Bridge and back. Spanning 2,053 feet and standing 301 feet high, the Kinzua Bridge is reputed to be the second highest railroad viaduct in the United States. The train runs Friday, Saturday, and Sunday during June and September; every day except Mondays during July and August; Wednesday through Sunday during the first two weeks of October (prime foliage season for the area) and weekends only during the last half of October. The round-trip is $20 for adults; $13 for children ages three to twelve.

Another highlight of the Allegheny National Forest is the **Flying W Ranch,** west of Marienville in Tionesta. This 500-acre working ranch sits within the boundaries of the National Forest and offers countless opportunities for adventure. Spend an hour or a week here taking Western riding lessons, canoeing on the Allegheny River, hiking, fishing, and more. In July, come for the professional **Allegheny Mountain Championship Rodeo.** For a real adventure, go on one of the overnight horseback trips into the national forest.

Accommodations range from bunkhouses to cabins. Or, bring your RV and hook-up at the campground. In the summer, the ranch offers a Western riding camp for children ages nine through sixteen. For more information, call (814) 463–7663.

COOKSBURG

From Marienville, head south on Route 66 to **Cook Forest State Park** in Cooksburg. Not only does this area harbor one of the largest stands of virgin hemlock and pine forests in the East, it is also home to a thriving arts center. The combination is unbeatable for a family vacation.

Cook Forest Center for the Arts has a full schedule of art exhibits, demonstrations, classes, and festivals for all ages. In the summer, there's a children's program that meets for two hours a day, five days a week. Each day, the children make a different craft and learn about the arts or even recycling and the environment. There's a young peoples' drama workshop for a week each summer. Seven different festivals take place here during the season. One of the most popular is the Teddy Bear Weekend at the end of July. For information and a schedule of upcoming events, call (814) 927–6655 during May through September; (814) 744–9670 from October through April.

At the summer arts program sponsored by the Cook Forest Center for the Arts, children create tangible memories of their vacations. (Courtesy Cook Forest Center for the Arts)

Cook Forest State Park offers great hiking, canoeing, and fishing on the Clarion River, as well as bicycling and winter sports. There are camping and rustic cabins for rent within the park. Outside the park there are numerous choices for accommodations. For families who want to combine horseback-riding with their vacation, one of the best choices is the **Pine Crest Cabins.** Don't let the name fool you: There is a campground and stables on the property as well. There are also canoes, go-carts, bumper boats, and long-putt golf—all on a seventy-five-acre family oriented resort. More than half of the land has been preserved in its natural state and provides great hiking territory for families.

Horseback-riding runs about $13 for a one-hour tour; $22 for two hours. Camping starts at $12 a night for a primitive site; more if you want water or electric at the site. Log cabins sleep eight to ten people and run $75 a night; $400 per week. Each has an indoor and outdoor fireplace and two or three bedrooms. Call (814) 752–2200 for information and reservations.

If you want to see your wildlife up a little closer, check out the **Double Diamond Deer Ranch,** near the entrance to the State Park on Route 36 South. Here a herd of twenty deer have been raised since birth. The deer are tame, so they'll come right up and greet you, eat from your hand and enjoy a good scratch behind the ears. Fawns are born each spring, and during June through August they are bottle fed. Children are welcome to hold the bottles. To find out current hours and admission prices, call (814) 752–6334.

PUNXSUTAWNEY

Before heading west, drive south on Route 36 to Punxsutawney, one of Pennsylvania's most unusual towns.

On **Groundhog Day** each year, the world focuses its attention on the little town of Punxsutawney and on a groundhog named Phil. If he climbs out of his burrow on Gobbler's Knob and sees his shadow, the story goes, winter will be sticking around for a while longer. Phil's an old hand at this prediction stuff: He (or his descendants) has been doing it every year since February 2, 1887.

But you don't have to wait until February to get a glimpse of Phil. He can be found living with his family at **Phil's Zoo** at the Civic Complex in Punxsutawney. Each summer the town celebrates its favorite son with a week-long **Groundhog Festival** in July. Parades, dances, contests, flea markets, and lots of food are all part of the festivities.

Lest you think that groundhogs are all there is to Punxsutawney, check out the **Punxsutawney Historical and Genealogical Museum** (401 West Mahoning Street, 814–938–2555). Of course, a good bit of the museum is devoted to groundhog history and lore, but there are other treasures from the town's past as well.

Outside of town, stop by the **Coolspring Power Museum,** a collection of more than 250 internal combustion engines that trace the 110-year history of that important invention. Another fun stop is the **Historic Big Run Mill,** 6 miles from Punxsutawney on Route 119. This working mill was built in the 1860s and still grinds locally grown buckwheat into flour.

For more information on the sights and festivals of "The Weather Capital of the World," call the Punxsutawney Chamber of Commerce at (814) 938–7700.

OIL CITY AND TITUSVILLE

To get a better picture of the history of oil in this area, head to Oil City and Titusville. In Oil City, you can board the **Oil Creek & Titusville Railroad** through "the valley that changed the world." The two-and-a-half-hour narrated trip describes the world's first oil boom. The train runs Saturdays and Sundays from June through October with additional trains on Wednesdays, Thursdays, and Fridays during July, August, and October. Call ahead for fares and schedule information: (814) 676–1733.

Heading up Route 8 toward Titusville, stop at the **Drake Well Museum,** where Edwin Drake drilled the first oil well in 1859. Here you'll find displays recounting the history of oil in the area, as well as operating oil equipment. Trails along Oil Creek provide great hiking and there's a picnic pavilion. The park is open year-round, daily May though October, closed Mondays November through April. Admission charged. For more information, call (814) 827–2797.

In East Titusville on Dotyville Road, don't miss the **Otto Cupler Torpedo Company and Nitroglycerin Museum.** Weekends from June to October, there is a daily Nitroglycerin Special Effects Show that demonstrates the role nitroglycerin played in the area's oil fields starting in the 1870s. This company is the only oil well–shooting organization still in operation. Call ahead for information and schedules: (814) 827–2921.

GREENVILLE

From Titusville, take routes 8 and 417 to Franklin, then hop on Route 358 going west to Greenville. In town, there are a couple of museums worth a look-see. The **Canal Museum** at Lock 22 Alan Avenue traces the history of the Erie Extension Canal. You can see a full-sized replica of a packet boat and working model of a canal lock. Call (412) 588–7574 for hours and admission information. The **Greenville Railroad Park and Museum** is at 314 Main Street. Here your kids can climb aboard the largest switch engine ever built. Call (412) 588–4009 for more information.

If you're in town on a Wednesday or Saturday, check out the Greenville

Farmers' Curb Market at the corner of Penn Avenue and Main Street. It's open 7:00 A.M. to 2:00 P.M. and features the produce of farmers within a 20-mile radius of town.

Just south of town on Route 18, you'll find the **Brucker Great Blue Heron Sanctuary,** where more than 400 of these majestic birds nest. It's the largest colony of herons in the state. Admission is free.

The Shenango Conservancy has preserved several remnants of the Erie Extension Canal in Mercer County, including **Lock #10, Kidd's Mill Covered Bridge,** and the **Shenango Trail.** The 8-mile trail follows the towpath of the canal and its a great place for an easy family hike. For more information on these historic attractions, contact the Shenango Conservancy, 94 East Shenango Street, Sharpsville 16150 or call (412) 981–0543.

SHARON AND HERMITAGE

Chocolate lovers will want to stop by two unusual factories in the towns of Sharon and Hermitage, both south of Greenville on Route 62.

At 496 East State Street in Sharon, **Daffin's Candies Chocolate Kingdom** is a sight to behold. The display area is filled with giant rabbits, turtles, elephants, and more—all made of chocolate. The rabbit alone required 700 pounds of chocolate to create! If you make arrangements in advance, you can tour the chocolate factory, located on Route 60, south of Sharon. Call (412) 342–2892 for more information.

In Hermitage, tour the 30,000-square-foot facility at **Philadelphia Candies,** a company that's been making fine chocolates and other confections since 1919. The retail store is located right at the factory so you can bring home a sample for all your friends back home (if the candies make it that far!). Philadelphia Candies is located at 1546 State Street in Hermitage. Call (412) 981–6341 for more information.

Before you leave Hermitage, take a walk down the **Avenue of Flags.** The street is lined with 444 flags, making it the world's largest display of American flags. The visitor's center is at 2634 East State Street. For more information, call (412) 346–0444 or (800) 621–6744.

JAMESTOWN

North of Greenville on Route 58, Jamestown is the gateway to **Pymatuning State Park** and home to Pennsylvania's largest manmade lake. With the 27-square-mile lake as its centerpiece, the park offers boating, hiking, fishing, camping, and winter sports. Call (412) 932–3141 for more information.

While in Jamestown, make a point to stop by the **Pymatuning Deer**

FAITH AND EMILY'S FAVORITE EVENTS IN CENTRAL AND NORTHWESTERN PENNSYLVANIA

PA Cross-Country Sled Dog Championship (late January) Marshburg (814) 368–9370

Kid Connection (late April) Lewistown (717) 784–2522

American Folkways Festival (mid-June and beginning of September) Clintonville (814) 385–6040

Erie Summer Festival of the Arts (late June) Erie (814) 864–0191 or 833–0812

Central Pennsylvania Festival of the Arts (mid-July) State College (814) 237–3682

Ag Progress Days (mid-August) State College (814) 865–2081

Park, also on Route 58. This small zoo offers train and pony rides. Small children especially seem to enjoy this stop. For hours and admission information, call (412) 932–3200.

ERIE

Drive east on Route 58 and get the express road (Route 79) to Erie, a city that combines family-friendly attractions with the lure of one of the Great Lakes.

Presque Isle State Park is one of the most remarkable aspects of the city. This narrow spit of sand (*presque isle* literally means "almost an island") juts out into Lake Erie, providing an unusual environment for wildlife and a beautiful retreat for humans.

Beaches line each side of the peninsula. Choose the calm waters of Presque Isle Bay or the almost ocean-like waves of Lake Erie. Water enthusiasts can rent canoes, rowboats, or motorboats to explore the waters on their own while landlubbers can enjoy 7 miles of hiking trails. Bring your binoculars; Presque Isle is touted as one of the best bird-watching sites in the country. To plan your day at the park, stop at the visitor's center.

Although busiest in summer, there's something to do year-round at the park. In the winter, hiking trails turn to cross-country ski trails and Presque Isle

Bay provides great ice-fishing. For more information about the park, call (814) 838–8776.

Right outside the entrance of the park is **Waldameer Park and Water World.** If you don't spot it, your kids definitely will. With eleven slides (five for little ones), three "tad pool" areas, a heated pool, ferris wheel, train rides, roller coaster, and carousel, every family can find something to like about the park. Use of tubes and life jackets is free, and there is a variety of restaurants, snack bars, and concessions at the park. Or you can bring your own picnic. Puppet shows are offered throughout the day. The park is open Tuesday through Sunday from mid-May to Labor Day. Call ahead for hours and admission fees: (814) 838–3591.

The bayfront area of downtown Erie holds a number of other maritime attractions. At the foot of State Street, you can take a look at the *Wolverine*— at least what's left of it. The ship, originally christened the U.S.S. Michigan, was the first iron-hulled ship ever built. Now the bow is all that remains of this impressive part of maritime history.

At the foot of Holland Street, you can tour the Flagship *Niagara,* a schooner built to fight the naval battles of the War of 1812. When the ship is in port, it is open for tours, Monday through Saturday from 9:00 A.M. to 5:00 P.M. and Sunday noon to 5:00 P.M. To avoid disappointing children with their hearts set on seeing this boat, call ahead: (814) 871–4596.

At the end of East Sixth Street, on Lighthouse Street, take a tour of the **Land Lighthouse,** built in 1813. While there, climb to the top of the cliff and take in a wonderful view of Lake Erie.

There are several sights in downtown Erie that are especially good for children. Aspiring firefighters will want to check out the **Firefighters Historical Museum** (428 Chestnut Street; 814–456–5969) housed in an old firehouse. You can examine firefighting equipment that dates back as far as 1823. The 1927 La France firetruck will be a hit with kids. The museum is open weekends only. Admission is free.

Star gazers should head for the **Gannon University Planetarium,** part of the Gannon University Historical Museum housed in the Watson/Curtze Mansion. The planetarium offers shows Thursday through Saturday at 2:00 P.M., Sunday at 2:00 P.M. and 3:00 P.M. Additional shows may be offered during the summer months. Call (814) 871–5794 for more information.

For small children, however, the highlight of Erie is the newly opened **ExpERIEnce Children's Museum,** housed in an old livery stable at 420 French Street. According to one of the museum's curators, "This is a hands-on museum. Which means that kids can come in and break things, and after they leave we fix them." There's a Gallery of Science on one floor and a Gallery of the Human Experience on the other. You can also see a simulation of a cave, in which children learn about cave painting, cave exploration, and fossils. At the Wegman's Corner Store, children can shop in a re-creation of a supermarket, complete with scanners, shopping carts, and very real-looking groceries. Youngsters may want to pick out a funny outfit from the costume closet and put on a show on a real stage.

The museum is aimed at kids ages two to twelve, but those under age eight seem to enjoy it the most. The museum is open year-round, 10:00 A.M. to 4:00 P.M. Wednesday through Saturday and 1:00 to 4:00 P.M. on Sunday. Admission is $3.50 for adults and children over age two. Family memberships are available.

NORTHEAST

About 20 miles east of Erie on Route 20 is the historic village of Northeast. Take a walking tour of the historic district (brochures are available at local stores and museums). A highlight for children is the **Hornby School Museum,** a restored one-room schoolhouse originally built in the 1870s. If you call ahead and make arrangements, your children can experience what it was like to learn in a one-room schoolhouse. Open Sundays from 1:00 to 5:00 P.M., June through October. Call (814) 725–5680 for tour information.

Another historical sight of interest to children is the **Lake Shore Railway Historical Society Museum.** Here, at the corner of Wall and Robinson streets, you can see a variety of train equipment, including a pullman car, caboose, and dining car. Located on a busy stretch of railroad track, the site practically guarantees that your children will get to see several modern trains pass by during your visit. The museum is open Wednesday through Sunday 1:00 to 5:00 P.M. from Memorial Day to Labor Day, weekends only during September and October. Call (814) 825–2724 or 725–1191 for more information.

GENERAL INDEX

ACTIVITIES INDEX

MUSIC

NATURE AND NATURE CENTERS

OFF-BEAT AND UNUSUAL

PARKS & GARDENS

PLAYGROUNDS

RESORTS & HOTELS

Flyers, 20
Forbes Field, 98
Greenberg Indoor Sports Complex, 137
Lackawanna County Stadium, 122
Nittany Lions, 138
Penguins, 98
Phantoms, 98
Phillies, 20
Pirates, 98
Red Barons, 122
Riverfront Park, 60
Riverside Stadium, 60
76ers, 20
Steelers, 98
Stingers, 98
Three Rivers Stadium, 98
Veterans Stadium, 20
Wings, 20

THEME AND AMUSEMENT PARKS
Bland's Park, 80
Caddie Shak, Inc., 73
Carousel Water & Fun Park, 118
Dorney Park and Wildwater Kingdom, 41–42
Dutch Wonderland Family Fun Park, 53
Hersheypark, 56
Idlewild Park, 74
Kennywood Park, 99–100
Knoebel's Amusement Park and Campground, 131
Lakemont Park, 82
Sandcastle Action Park, 100
Sandcastle Waterpark, 100
Shawnee Place Play and Water Park, 111
Terry Hill Waterpark, 43

TOURIST INFORMATION
Ask the Amish, 45
Brandywine Valley Tourist Information Center, 23
Bureau of Forestry, 136
Endless Mountains Visitors Bureau, 127
Lawrence County Tourist Promotion Agency, 106
Lion Country Convention and Visitors Bureau, 136
National Park Service, 3, 117
Nazareth Area Visitors Center, 43
New Hope Information Center, 34
Northeast Territory Visitor's Bureau, 123
Pennsylvania Dutch Convention and Visitors Bureau, 46
Philadelphia convention and Visitor's Bureau, 1
Punxsutawney Chamber of Commerce, 148
State Park Information, 127
Sullivan County Chamber of Commerce, 127
Union County Tourist Agency, 132
Upper Delaware Council, 117–18
Village of New Hope, 34
Wayne County Chamber of Commerce, 119

TOURS
American Trolley Tours/Choo-Choo Trolley, 1
Amish Country Tours, 51
Ben Franklin Carriage Co/'76 Carriage Co., 1
Gray Line Tours, 3

ABOUT THE AUTHORS

Both Emily and Faith Paulsen live in Pennsylvania. Emily is a soon-to-be mother and an experienced travel writer and editor who writes regularly for *FamilyTimes*, *The Scranton Times*, and other publications. Faith is the mother of three boys and a freelance writer whose articles have appeared in the *Philadelphia Sun* and *Physician Lifestyle Magazine*, as well as other publications. Both sisters devote much of their time together discovering the many family-friendly attractions in Pennsylvania